Toolkit for Democracy

Empower, Act, Transform: A Step-by-Step Blueprint for Real-World Activism

Jacob Baxter-Wyatt

Table of Contents

INTRODUCTION

Have you ever felt frustrated watching the news, wishing you could do something to change the narrative? What if I told you that your voice holds the power to reshape your community? These questions might seem daunting at first glance, but they are the starting point for an essential journey of civic engagement. In our current political landscape, where disillusionment and apathy often dominate, it's easy to feel powerless. However, it's precisely during these times that active participation becomes crucial. Democracy, at its core, relies on the voices and actions of its citizens. Every email sent, every protest attended, and every vote cast contribute to shaping the future we all share.

Civic engagement is not just a lofty ideal; it's a practical necessity that influences our day-to-day lives. From local policies that affect our schools and neighborhoods to national decisions with far-reaching impacts, our involvement can bring about meaningful change. Yet, many people feel disconnected from the political process, unsure of where to begin or how to make their voices heard. This book aims to bridge that gap by providing clear guidance and actionable steps that anyone, regardless of background or experience, can follow to become an engaged and effective participant in their community.

Reflecting on my own journey, I recall the first time I attended a town hall meeting. Initially, I was intimidated by the thought of speaking up among experienced activists and community leaders. But as I listened and absorbed the discussions, I realized that my perspective was valuable. When I finally mustered the courage to ask a question, it sparked a conversation that led to tangible changes in our neighborhood. That experience was transformative, highlighting the power of individual action within a collective setting. It proved to me that even small contributions can lead to significant outcomes.

This book is designed with three primary audiences in mind. First, it speaks to young adults and university students who are passionate about social issues but uncertain about how to channel that passion into action. For this group, the book offers foundational knowledge and practical tips to get started in activism. Secondly, it aims to support community leaders and organizers seeking to enhance their skills in networking, advocacy, and event planning to mobilize grassroots efforts effectively. For these readers, the book provides advanced strategies and insights to refine their approaches and expand their impact. Finally, it addresses citizens who have previously been disengaged from political processes but are now motivated to participate meaningfully in civic activities. This audience will find encouragement and step-by-step guidance to overcome initial barriers and become active contributors to democratic dialogue.

Each chapter of this book is structured to build on the last, creating a comprehensive toolkit that evolves with the reader's growing understanding and confidence. We begin with the basics of why civic engagement matters, outlining the historical context and current relevance of active participation. Subsequent chapters delve into specific areas such as understanding the political landscape, identifying key issues, and leveraging social media for advocacy. Practical exercises are included throughout to help readers apply what they've learned in real-world scenarios. Whether it's drafting a compelling email to a local representative, organizing a community meeting, or launching a campaign on social media, the book offers concrete steps to turn knowledge into action.

Moreover, the book emphasizes the importance of building and nurturing networks. Effective civic engagement doesn't happen in isolation; it's strengthened through relationships and collective effort. We'll explore strategies for connecting with like-minded individuals, forming alliances, and collaborating on initiatives. By working together, we can amplify our voices and achieve more significant results than any one person could alone.

The road to becoming an engaged citizen can be challenging, filled with obstacles and moments of doubt. But it's also incredibly rewarding, offering a sense of purpose and connection to something larger than oneself. Throughout this book, you'll find stories of everyday people who stepped out of their comfort zones and made a difference. These narratives serve as both inspiration and proof that significant change begins with ordinary individuals taking small, deliberate actions.

As you navigate through the chapters, you'll gradually build a robust set of skills and a deeper understanding of how to effect change. From mastering the art of persuasive communication to organizing impactful events, each lesson is designed to empower you to take proactive steps toward reshaping your community and beyond. The tools and strategies provided are not only practical but adaptable, allowing you to tailor them to your unique environment and goals.

In conclusion, this book is more than just a guide; it's an invitation to embark on a journey of empowerment and transformation. Whether you're a student eager to address social injustices, a community leader aiming to galvanize local efforts, or a citizen ready to engage politically for the first time, this book equips you with the knowledge and confidence to make your voice heard. Remember, the strength of a democracy lies in the active participation of its citizens. Your voice matters, and together, we can create a more just and equitable world. So let's begin this journey, one step at a time, towards becoming informed, engaged, and empowered participants in our democracy.

CHAPTER 1

The Essenceof Civic Engagement

Civic engagement serves as the backbone of a democratic society. It represents the actions individuals and groups take, aimed at contributing to the communal well-being and enhancing civic life. These activities strengthen communities and foster a more inclusive society. For young adults, community leaders, and previously disengaged citizens, understanding civic engagement is key to making a meaningful impact.

In this chapter, we will explore the definition and scope of civic engagement, highlighting its various forms such as voting, local activism, community service, and advocacy. We will delve into examples that illustrate how these actions collectively contribute to shaping public policies and fostering a culture of accountability. Additionally, the role of civic education in equipping individuals with the knowledge needed for effective participation will be examined. By the end, readers will grasp the multifaceted nature of civic engagement and its significance in building robust, equitable communities.

Definition and Scope of Civic Engagement

Civic engagement can be seen as the backbone of a democratic society. It involves both individual and collective actions aimed at contributing to communal well-being and improving civic life. These actions are the building blocks that foster stronger communities and promote a more inclusive society. Understanding the role of civic engagement is critical for young adults, community leaders, and even previously disengaged citizens who are keen on making a meaningful impact.

To begin with, let's define what civic engagement entails. Civic engagement encompasses both personal and group efforts aimed at tackling public issues and enabling communities to achieve better outcomes for all members. This is not limited to high-profile political activities; it also includes everyday actions like participating in local meetings, volunteering, or even simply being informed about community happenings. The core idea is involvement—taking responsibility for and actively participating in one's community.

One of the most common forms of civic engagement is voting. Voting is a powerful tool that gives individuals a direct voice in selecting leaders and shaping policies that affect their lives. It's a fundamental way for citizens to express their preferences and hold elected officials accountable. Encouraging young adults to vote ensures that diverse voices are represented in decision-making processes, which can result in more equitable and inclusive policies.

Local activism is another significant aspect of civic engagement. This involves rallying around specific issues affecting a community, whether it's advocating for better schooling, improved public transportation, or environmental protections. Local activists often work through petitions, town hall meetings, and community boards to influence changes. Their efforts help to spotlight issues that might otherwise be overlooked by larger governmental entities, ensuring those in power address them.

Community service also plays a crucial role in civic engagement. Activities such as organizing neighborhood clean-ups, running food drives, or mentoring youth programs strengthen social bonds and create a sense of belonging among community members. These efforts not only resolve immediate needs but also build long-term resilience within communities. Volunteering fosters empathy and teaches invaluable skills, making it an essential component of an engaged and vibrant society.

Advocacy is another impactful form of civic engagement. Advocacy goes beyond addressing immediate concerns to influencing broader policy and institutional change. This could involve lobbying government officials, creating awareness campaigns, or participating in civil demonstrations. Advocates champion causes ranging from human rights to environmental conservation. By drawing attention to important issues and proposing solutions, advocacy helps ensure that all voices, especially marginalized ones, are heard.

A critical element that fortifies all these forms of civic engagement is civic education. Civic education equips individuals with the knowledge they need about their rights, responsibilities, and the workings of their government. Schools play a vital role here by integrating civics into their curriculums, teaching students not only about historical governance but also about contemporary societal issues and how to engage with them. Knowledgeable citizens are more likely to participate effectively in civic activities and contribute thoughtfully to public discourse.

The importance of civic education extends beyond just knowing one's rights; it also focuses on understanding responsibilities. This includes recognizing the significance of paying taxes, obeying the law, serving on juries, and participating in public debates. When people understand their roles within the larger framework of society, they are more inclined to take steps that benefit the collective good.

Active participation in civic life can substantially shape policies and foster a culture of accountability. When citizens come together to address community issues, their collective action can bring about significant policy changes. For example, grassroots mobilization has led to groundbreaking legislation on various fronts such as civil rights, environmental protection, and healthcare reforms. This type of engagement ensures that the government remains accountable to its citizens and acts in their best interests.

A culture of accountability thrives when there are mechanisms for feedback and redress. Civic engagement provides platforms for citizens to voice their concerns and hold policymakers responsible for their actions. Public forums, social media campaigns, and watchdog organizations are just a few examples of how engaged citizens can keep their leaders in check. This oversight leads to more transparent and responsive governance, which is essential for a healthy democracy.

Moreover, fostering a culture of accountability encourages public trust in institutions. When people see that their participation yields results, they are more likely to remain engaged and encourage others to join in. Trust in public institutions is often a precursor to increased civic participation, creating a virtuous cycle wherein engagement and accountability reinforce each other.

In summary, civic engagement is multifaceted, involving a range of activities from voting and activism to community service and advocacy. Each form of engagement plays a unique role in enhancing community life and ensuring that democratic principles are upheld. Civic education is the cornerstone that empowers individuals with the knowledge and tools needed for effective participation. Active involvement in civic activities shapes policies and promotes a culture of accountability, ultimately leading to a more robust and equitable society. By understanding and embracing the various aspects of civic engagement, young adults, community leaders, and previously disengaged citizens can find meaningful ways to contribute to the greater good.

Historical Examples of Effective Civic Participation

One of the most striking examples of civic engagement in American history is the Civil Rights Movement of the 1960s. This movement was a powerful demonstration of how grassroots activism could lead to significant societal change. Activists from diverse backgrounds united with a shared goal: to end racial segregation and discrimination against African Americans. They organized sit-ins, marches, and boycotts, which drew national attention to their cause. The impact was profound, leading to landmark legislation such as the Civil Rights Act of 1964 and the Voting Rights Act of 1965. These laws dismantled legal segregation and ensured voting rights for all citizens, forever changing the social fabric of the United States.

Shifting our focus to another pivotal moment in history, the Women's Suffrage Movement stands out as a testament to perseverance and resilience. For decades, women fought tirelessly for the right to vote, facing immense opposition and numerous setbacks. Leaders like Susan B. Anthony and Elizabeth Cady Stanton formed organizations, held conventions, and lobbied government officials to advocate for women's voting rights. Their relentless efforts culminated in the passage of the 19th Amendment in 1920, granting women the right to vote. This achievement not only transformed the political landscape but also inspired future generations to continue fighting for gender equality in all spheres of life.

Environmental advocacy has also played a crucial role in shaping legislative actions aimed at preserving our planet. The first Earth Day, celebrated on April 22, 1970, marked a turning point in environmental awareness. Millions of people across the United States participated in rallies and educational events, highlighting the urgent need to protect the environment. This widespread civic engagement led to significant legislative achievements, including the establishment of the Environmental Protection Agency (EPA) and the passage of the Clean Air Act. These measures have had lasting effects, improving air quality and setting the stage for future environmental protections.

Local initiatives provide another compelling example of how community organizing can lead to meaningful change. Across the country, countless communities have mobilized to address local issues and improve the quality of life for their residents. One such instance is the fight for affordable housing in urban areas. Community organizers have worked together to advocate for policies that ensure access to safe and affordable housing for all citizens. Through petitions, public meetings, and partnerships with local government officials, these grassroots efforts have resulted in the development of affordable housing projects and the implementation of tenant protection laws. These local victories demonstrate the power of civic engagement in addressing specific community needs and fostering a sense of unity and purpose among residents.

Types of Civic Engagement

Voting is a fundamental form of civic engagement that influences policy and leadership. Voting allows individuals to have a say in who represents them at various levels of government, from local officials to the president. This act of participation helps shape the direction of policies, laws, and community projects that impact everyday life. Voting empowers citizens to choose leaders who reflect their values and priorities, making it one of the most direct ways to influence governance. For instance, elected representatives create laws on education, healthcare, and taxation—areas that affect everyone. By voting, individuals can support candidates whose platforms align with their own views on these crucial issues.

Yet, voting is more than a simple right; it's a responsibility. Voters need to be informed about the candidates and the issues at stake. Numerous resources are available to help voters make educated decisions, such as voter guides and debates. Universities and community organizations often host events where candidates discuss their positions on various topics. Social media and online forums also provide platforms for political discussions, offering diverse perspectives. Being an informed voter means not just understanding one's own needs but also considering the broader community's welfare.

Volunteering in community service projects helps address local needs and build social cohesion. Volunteering can take many forms, from participating in a neighborhood cleanup to tutoring students or assisting in soup kitchens. These efforts contribute to the well-being of the community by addressing specific issues like food insecurity, education gaps, and environmental sustainability. When people come together to volunteer, they not only improve their surroundings but also build stronger relationships within the community. This social cohesion fosters a sense of belonging and mutual support, making communities more resilient.

For example, volunteering at a local food bank provides immediate relief to families facing hunger and encourages a culture of giving and empathy. Community service projects can also be an excellent way for young adults and university students to gain valuable experience and skills. These activities often require teamwork, problem-solving, and effective communication, all of which are transferable to various professional fields. Furthermore, volunteering offers a way to meet new people, network, and even discover career interests. Many find that their passion for a cause leads them to a fulfilling career in non-profit work or community organizing.

Participating in public meetings and advocacy campaigns allows citizens to voice their concerns. Public meetings, such as city council sessions and school board meetings, offer forums where individuals can express their opinions directly to decision-makers. Advocacy campaigns, on the other hand, often involve petitions, rallies, and social media outreach to bring attention to specific causes. Both forms of engagement are essential for holding officials accountable and ensuring diverse voices are heard in the policymaking process.

Public meetings provide a structured environment for dialogue between officials and constituents. For those new to civic engagement, attending a meeting can be eye-opening, revealing how decisions are made and who the key players are. Speaking at these meetings requires preparation and confidence, but even listening can be informative. Residents might learn about upcoming projects, zoning changes, or budget allocations that directly affect their lives. Advocacy campaigns often focus on broader issues, like climate change, healthcare reform, or social justice. These campaigns unite people with shared concerns and amplify their collective voice. Organizers often use technology and social media to coordinate efforts, mobilize supporters, and spread information quickly.

Each form of engagement offers unique opportunities to influence community change. While voting impacts who makes decisions, volunteering and public meetings allow citizens to influence what those decisions will be and how they are implemented. Together, these forms of civic engagement create a comprehensive approach to community involvement, ensuring that individuals can participate in ways that match their skills, interests, and levels of commitment.

For example, someone passionate about environmental issues might start by voting for candidates with strong environmental policies. They could then volunteer for a local cleanup project and attend city council meetings to advocate for better waste management practices. This multi-faceted approach not only maximizes their impact but also keeps them engaged in the long term. Each action reinforces the other, creating a cycle of ongoing participation and influence.

Current Challenges in Civic Activism

In today's democratic society, civic engagement is essential yet faces numerous contemporary challenges that need to be analyzed for better understanding and action. One of the primary barriers to robust civic participation is apathy. Many citizens feel disconnected from political processes or believe their involvement will not make a substantial difference. This sense of disillusionment can lead to widespread disengagement, weakening the pillars of democracy. Misinformation also poses a significant challenge by distorting facts and fostering distrust. When people are inundated with false information, it becomes increasingly difficult for them to make informed decisions, which further hampers meaningful engagement.

Technology, while often hailed as a tool for facilitating mobilization, is a double-edged sword. On one hand, social media and other digital platforms provide unprecedented opportunities to organize, communicate, and mobilize. Campaigns can go viral in hours, reaching a vast audience and galvanizing support at an extraordinary pace. For example, movements like Black Lives Matter have effectively used technology to raise awareness and rally supporters worldwide. However, these same platforms can contribute to polarization. Algorithms designed to maximize engagement often promote sensationalist content, which can include misinformation. This creates echo chambers where users are exposed only to viewpoints that reinforce their existing beliefs, making constructive dialogue more challenging.

Despite these obstacles, emerging movements offer a beacon of hope by showcasing new approaches to grassroots organizing. The Fight for $15 movement, which advocates for raising the minimum wage to $15 per hour, illustrates how dedicated activism can lead to tangible change. What began as a small group of workers demanding higher wages has grown into a national campaign, influencing policy changes in various states and cities. This movement emphasizes the power of persistent, organized efforts and demonstrates that collective action can yield significant results even in the face of systemic resistance.

Coalition-building across diverse groups presents both challenges and opportunities for broader impact. Effective coalitions bring together various stakeholders, each with unique perspectives and resources, to work towards common goals. For instance, environmental organizations might collaborate with labor unions to address climate justice, blending environmental concerns with workers' rights. While such alliances can amplify the impact of advocacy efforts, they also require navigating complex dynamics and potential conflicts. Different groups may have varying priorities and methods, necessitating careful coordination and compromise. Nevertheless, when done successfully, coalition-building can create a more inclusive and powerful force for change.

These contemporary challenges and opportunities underscore the need for strategic, informed actions to enhance civic engagement. Addressing apathy involves education and empowerment. Schools, community organizations, and leaders must emphasize the importance of civic participation and provide accessible avenues for involvement. Creating spaces for open, factual discussions can counteract the effects of misinformation, enabling individuals to engage with issues critically. Technology must be leveraged responsibly, promoting initiatives that foster genuine connections and informed debate rather than division.

Broader Implications and Role of Education

In our democratic society, civic engagement plays a vital role in maintaining and improving the well-being of our communities. One of the most significant benefits of civic engagement is its ability to strengthen community cohesion. When individuals come together to address common issues or work on community projects, a sense of belonging and mutual responsibility develops. This not only improves relationships among community members but also fosters an environment where individuals are more likely to support one another. As a result, neighborhoods become safer, more vibrant places to live, and the overall quality of life improves.

Furthermore, civic engagement can lead to enhanced public policies. When citizens participate in local government meetings, contribute to public discussions, or engage in advocacy, they influence decision-making processes. Their input helps ensure that policies reflect the needs and desires of the community. Engaging with policymakers can also hold them accountable, leading to more transparent and effective governance. For instance, when residents organize around issues like clean water or safe parks, their collective voice can prompt lawmakers to take meaningful action.

Education is another critical component in nurturing engaged citizens. It fosters critical thinking and raises awareness about societal issues, enabling people to make informed decisions and take effective actions. Educational institutions play a crucial role by incorporating civic education into their curricula. Programs that teach students about their rights and responsibilities as citizens, the functioning of government, and the importance of participation lay the groundwork for lifelong civic engagement. Schools that encourage debates, discussions, and active involvement instill in students the skills and motivation needed to engage with civic issues confidently.

Moreover, education helps individuals understand the complexities of societal problems and equips them with the tools to address these challenges thoughtfully. For example, courses on environmental science can raise awareness about climate change, prompting students to get involved in sustainability initiatives. Similarly, history classes that cover social movements can inspire students to advocate for justice and equality. By fostering a deeper understanding of societal issues, education empowers individuals to contribute meaningfully to their communities.

Strong civic participation also deters apathy and promotes a culture of accountability. When citizens actively participate in civic activities, it creates a ripple effect that encourages others to join in. This collective involvement reduces feelings of helplessness and disengagement, countering the apathy that often plagues modern societies. An active citizenry keeps elected officials and institutions accountable, ensuring they serve the public's best interests. For example, voter turnout is a critical measure of democratic health. High voter participation signals to politicians that the electorate is attentive and invested in their performance, pushing them to be more responsive and responsible.

Creating a culture of accountability begins with understanding that every action, no matter how small, contributes to broader societal change. Volunteering at a local food bank, attending town hall meetings, or even participating in online discussions about policy matters can collectively shape the community's future. When citizens consistently hold their leaders accountable through various forms of engagement, it leads to more ethical leadership and better governance.

Civic education is indispensable in preparing citizens to participate meaningfully in democracy. From a young age, formal and informal educational settings should aim to cultivate an appreciation for democratic values and processes. Lessons on how government systems work, the significance of voting, and the impact of individual and collective action help build a foundation for informed and active citizenship. Teachers should encourage students to think critically about current events, understand the implications of public policies, and develop strong communication and advocacy skills.

Extracurricular activities also offer valuable opportunities for civic learning. Participating in student government, service clubs, or community outreach programs provides practical experience in leadership, teamwork, and problem-solving—skills that translate directly into effective civic participation. These experiences help demystify the political process, making it more accessible and less intimidating for young people.

Additionally, fostering a habit of civic engagement from an early age increases the likelihood of continued involvement throughout adulthood. When individuals grow up understanding the importance and impact of their participation, they are more likely to remain engaged and motivated to contribute to their communities. Creating pathways for young adults to transition into more significant roles in civic organizations or local government further strengthens democratic participation.

Summary and Reflections

This chapter has delved into the significance of civic engagement and its various forms, such as voting, local activism, community service, and advocacy. Each of these activities plays a vital role in strengthening communities and promoting democratic values. By participating in these efforts, individuals contribute to creating more inclusive and resilient societies. The importance of civic education also stands out, equipping citizens with the necessary knowledge and skills to engage effectively and responsibly in public life.

Understanding and embracing civic engagement allows young adults, community leaders, and previously disengaged citizens to make meaningful contributions to their communities. Active participation not only helps shape policies but also fosters a culture of accountability and trust in public institutions. Through informed and engaged citizenry, we can ensure that our democratic society remains robust, equitable, and responsive to the needs of all its members.

CHAPTER 2

Building Effective Activist Networks

B uilding effective activist networks is essential for creating lasting social change. Strengthening these networks involves understanding key strategies that foster collaboration and communication among activists. Doing so enhances the collective impact of their efforts, making it more likely to achieve their shared goals. Activist networks thrive on mutual support, a sense of community, and clear guiding principles, all of which help unify diverse groups around common causes.

In this chapter, we will explore various strategies for recruiting like-minded individuals, including identifying core values and utilizing diverse outreach methods. We'll discuss the importance of maintaining effective communication within networks by setting clear protocols, using modern collaboration tools, and encouraging open feedback. Additionally, we'll delve into the role of digital platforms in expanding activist reach and engagement. Finally, we will examine techniques for sustaining long-term motivation and involvement by recognizing contributions, offering continuing education, and fostering a supportive community. These elements combined contribute to building robust and resilient activist networks capable of driving significant social change.

Recruiting Like-Minded Individuals

Identifying and bringing together individuals who share common values and goals for civic engagement is a crucial first step in building effective activist networks. To start, it's essential to identify and communicate the core values that unify your cause. Shared values act as the glue that binds people together, creating a sense of belonging and shared purpose. For instance, if your network aims to advocate for environmental sustainability, clearly articulate your commitment to this cause, emphasizing aspects such as reducing carbon footprints, promoting recycling programs, or supporting renewable energy initiatives. When potential members understand and resonate with these values, they are more likely to join and actively participate.

Once you have a clear understanding of your core values, diverse outreach strategies become vital to attract a wide range of supporters. Employing various methods will help you reach different demographics and communities. Hosting community events is a powerful way to engage directly with people in your locality. These could include town hall meetings, panel discussions, or educational seminars where you discuss your cause and how others can get involved. Social media also plays a significant role in modern activism. Platforms like Facebook, Twitter, and Instagram enable you to share your message widely and connect with individuals who might not be reachable through traditional means. Create engaging content, such as infographics, videos, and personal stories that highlight your cause's impact. Additionally, word-of-mouth remains a timeless strategy. Encourage current members to talk about the network and invite their friends and family to join.

Engagement through events is another impactful strategy to bring individuals together and foster strong connections. Organizing workshops, forums, or casual meet-ups provides opportunities for members to interact, exchange ideas, and build relationships. Workshops can focus on skill-building activities relevant to your cause, such as training sessions on public speaking, organizing rallies, or using social media effectively. Forums offer a platform for open discussions, enabling participants to share their experiences, challenges, and successes. Casual meet-ups, like coffee mornings or picnics, create a relaxed atmosphere where members can bond on a personal level. These events not only strengthen the sense of community but also keep the momentum going by maintaining high levels of enthusiasm and involvement.

A critical aspect of sustaining an activist network is follow-up and inclusion. It is important to regularly check in with new recruits to ensure they remain engaged and feel valued. This can be achieved through simple gestures like sending welcome messages, personalized emails, or newsletters that update them on recent activities and upcoming events. Establish a mentorship program where seasoned activists provide guidance and support to newcomers. Regularly solicit feedback from members to understand their needs and preferences better. This inclusive approach ensures that everyone feels heard and appreciated, which is essential for long-term commitment.

Effective Communication Within Networks

Effective communication is the backbone of any strong activist network. It serves as a foundation that ensures all members are on the same page, can collaborate effectively, and push towards common goals with unity. This subpoint will delve into various strategies to create these open and strategic communication channels that underpin successful activism.

One of the first steps in building these channels is establishing clear protocols. These guidelines promote transparency and accountability among network members. Transparency means that everyone within the network has access to the same information and understands processes clearly. For instance, if there are specific actions planned or decisions being made, they should be documented and accessible to all. Accountability, on the other hand, ensures that every member knows their roles and responsibilities and is answerable for their actions. A simple way to start is by creating a shared document that outlines these protocols, making it easy for everyone to refer back to them when needed. Regularly reviewing and updating this document can also help keep everyone aligned with the network's evolving needs and goals.

Utilizing collaboration tools is another essential practice in maintaining effective communication within activist networks. In the age of digital technology, numerous tools can streamline communication, making it easier for members to stay connected and organized. Group chats on platforms like WhatsApp or Telegram allow for instant messaging and quick updates. Forums and message boards provide a space for more in-depth discussions and idea exchanges. Project management platforms like Trello or Asana can help keep track of tasks and deadlines, ensuring everyone knows what they're working on and what needs attention next. By leveraging these tools, the network can avoid miscommunication and ensure that vital information doesn't get lost in translation.

Encouraging open feedback within the network is crucial for capturing diverse perspectives and refining approaches. An environment where feedback is welcomed and valued allows members to voice their ideas, concerns, and suggestions freely. This not only fosters a sense of belonging but also helps improve the network's strategies and activities. To encourage open feedback, regular check-ins and reflective sessions can be implemented. For example, setting up monthly meetings where members can share what's working well and what could be improved creates a structured opportunity for feedback. Additionally, anonymous surveys can be conducted to gather honest opinions without the fear of judgment. By doing so, the network can continuously evolve and adapt, making it more resilient and effective.

Crafting compelling updates is another way to maintain enthusiasm and focus within the network. Regular updates about the network's successes, challenges, and opportunities keep everyone informed and engaged. Sharing success stories, such as a successful rally or a milestone achieved, boosts morale and reinforces the purpose of the collective efforts. Highlighting challenges faced and how they were overcome demonstrates resilience and problem-solving capabilities, inspiring members to stay committed even during tough times. Moreover, communicating upcoming opportunities, like events or collaboration possibilities, keeps the momentum going and encourages active participation. Creating a newsletter or a dedicated update channel can be an effective way to disseminate these updates. Including visuals like photos or infographics makes the updates more engaging and relatable.

The importance of open and strategic communication channels cannot be overstated when building effective activist networks. Establishing clear protocols lays the groundwork for transparency and accountability, ensuring everyone is on the same page. Utilizing collaboration tools leverages modern technology to facilitate smooth and organized communication. Encouraging open feedback captures diverse perspectives, helping the network refine its approaches and remain adaptive. Crafting compelling updates maintains enthusiasm and focus, keeping all members motivated and informed.

Utilizing Digital Platforms for Expansion

Maximizing digital platforms to expand reach and strengthen activist networks is essential in today's interconnected world. Digital tools offer a unique opportunity to build, engage, and sustain powerful movements. This section provides insights into how young activists, community leaders, and previously disengaged citizens can utilize these platforms effectively.

One of the foundational steps to creating an effective activist network online is building a robust online presence. An engaging online identity through social media profiles and organizational websites significantly increases visibility. To begin with, it's vital to choose the right social media platforms where your target audience is most active. Platforms like Instagram, Twitter, Facebook, and TikTok each have their unique strengths. For example, Instagram's visual nature makes it perfect for sharing infographics and photos from events, while Twitter is excellent for real-time updates and short-form content. Creating a cohesive brand identity across these platforms helps establish trust and recognition. This includes using consistent logos, color schemes, and messaging that reflect the core values and objectives of your activism.

Developing a professional and regularly updated website also plays a critical role in your online presence. Your website serves as the central hub for all activities, providing detailed information about your mission, events, resources, and how new members can get involved. Essential elements of an effective website include an "About Us" section, a blog for posting updates and stories, contact information, and links to your social media channels. Additionally, having a mobile-friendly design ensures accessibility for all users, which is crucial for broadening your reach.

Once your online presence is established, leveraging social media for engagement becomes the next key focus. Social media channels are not just broadcasting tools but are powerful for fostering two-way conversations. Start by creating compelling content that encourages interaction. Pose questions to your followers, create polls, and invite them to share their thoughts on relevant issues. Engaging directly with comments and messages builds a sense of community and shows that every member's voice is valued. Consistent interaction nurtures loyalty and motivates supporters to participate more actively.

Regularly scheduled posts keep your audience informed and engaged. Use a content calendar to plan and organize your posts ahead of time, ensuring a mix of information, inspiration, and calls to action. For instance, you might share educational posts on Mondays, success stories on Wednesdays, and event reminders on Fridays. Visual content such as videos, infographics, and photos often garners more attention and shares than text-only posts, so incorporate visuals whenever possible.

Creating value-added content is another crucial component of strengthening your activist network online. Sharing valuable resources, educational materials, and success stories not only informs but inspires your network. Educational content can include articles, reports, how-to guides, and infographics related to the cause. For example, if your movement focuses on environmental activism, posting blogs about sustainable living tips or research findings on climate change can be highly impactful. Resourceful content positions your organization as a credible source of information and attracts individuals who want to learn more and contribute.

Additionally, highlighting success stories showcases the tangible impact of your efforts, motivating both current and potential supporters. Sharing testimonials from people who have benefited from your work or featuring interviews with prominent voices in your movement helps personalize your cause and foster deeper connections. Make sure to diversify the format of your content to cater to various preferences within your audience. Videos, podcasts, webinars, and written articles can all play a part in delivering value-added content.

Hosting virtual events is another powerful strategy for expanding reach and strengthening connections within your network. Virtual events such as webinars, panels, or online workshops enable you to engage with a broader audience regardless of geographical limitations. These events can serve multiple purposes—from educating participants about specific issues to mobilizing collective action.

Begin by identifying the topics that are most relevant and appealing to your audience. Inviting knowledgeable speakers or panelists who can provide expert insights adds credibility and draws in more participants. Promote your events well in advance through all your digital channels to maximize attendance. Create eye-catching promotional materials and share them frequently across your social media accounts, website, and email newsletters.

To ensure interactive and impactful virtual events, use technology that facilitates engagement. Platforms like Zoom, Google Meet, and Microsoft Teams offer features like Q&A sessions, breakout rooms, and polls that make events more interactive. Encourage attendees to ask questions, share their thoughts, and network with each other during these sessions. Recording these events and making them available on-demand extends their reach even further, allowing those who couldn't attend live to benefit from the content.

Sustaining Long-Term Engagement

Keeping activists motivated and involved over the long term is essential for the success and sustainability of activist networks. One effective strategy to achieve this involves recognizing contributions. Regular acknowledgment of efforts and achievements can significantly boost morale within the network. When members feel their hard work is appreciated, they are more likely to remain committed and engaged. Simple acts, such as verbal praise during meetings or highlighting successes in newsletters, can go a long way in making individuals feel valued. More formal recognition methods, like awards or certificates, can further reinforce the importance of each member's contribution.

Another key aspect of maintaining motivation is providing continuing education. Offering ongoing training and development opportunities helps keep skills sharp and knowledge current. For instance, organizing workshops, webinars, and courses on relevant topics ensures that activists stay informed about new strategies, tools, and trends. This not only enhances their effectiveness but also keeps them excited about their involvement. Additionally, partnering with experts and organizations outside the network can introduce fresh perspectives and ideas, enriching the learning experience for everyone involved.

Building a supportive community is also crucial in keeping activists engaged. A sense of camaraderie and mutual support can be a powerful antidote to burnout. Encouraging an environment where members feel comfortable sharing their experiences, challenges, and successes fosters deeper connections within the group. Activities like regular social gatherings, team-building exercises, and peer-mentoring programs can help strengthen these bonds. Furthermore, creating safe spaces for open dialogue allows members to express concerns and seek advice without fear of judgment.

Flexibility and adaptability are equally important in sustaining long-term involvement. The landscape of activism is constantly changing, and strategies that worked in the past may not always be effective. Being open to adjusting approaches as needed is vital for staying relevant and impactful. This might involve revisiting and refining goals, shifting focus areas, or adopting new technologies and methodologies. Engaging network members in these decisions can give them a sense of ownership and investment in the direction of their collective efforts. By fostering a culture of adaptability, the network can remain resilient in the face of evolving challenges.

Recognizing contributions begins with understanding that every effort, no matter how small, plays a role in advancing the cause. Publicly acknowledging these efforts can inspire others to contribute more actively. For example, creating a section in a monthly newsletter dedicated to 'Member Highlights' can showcase individual and group accomplishments. Social media shout-outs and blog posts celebrating milestones can also serve as public affirmations of appreciation. These gestures not only boost individual morale but also build a culture of gratitude within the network.

Continuing education should not be seen as a one-time event but as an ongoing commitment to growth. Organizers can develop annual training calendars, outlining various learning opportunities throughout the year. Topics could range from effective communication and negotiation skills to digital literacy and campaign management. Incorporating interactive elements such as Q&A sessions, group discussions, and hands-on activities can enhance engagement and retention of information. Additionally, providing access to online resources, e-books, and research articles can empower members to pursue self-directed learning.

A supportive community thrives on shared values and mutual respect. Establishing norms and guidelines that promote inclusivity and cooperation is fundamental. For instance, setting up a buddy system where experienced members mentor newcomers can ease the transition and foster a welcoming atmosphere. Regular check-ins and feedback sessions can help identify any issues early on and address them promptly. Celebrating personal milestones, such as birthdays or anniversaries, can also contribute to a sense of belonging and care within the network.

Adaptability requires a willingness to experiment and learn from experiences. Encouraging a mindset of continuous improvement can drive innovation and resilience. Setting up pilot projects or trial runs before fully implementing new initiatives allows for testing and adjustments based on feedback. Creating avenues for members to propose and lead new projects can harness diverse talents and perspectives, enhancing the network's overall capacity for change. Documenting lessons learned and sharing them widely ensures that valuable insights are retained and built upon.

Maintaining motivation over the long term is not just about grand gestures but also about consistent, everyday practices. Simple habits like starting meetings with positive updates, using inclusive language, and being prompt in communication can create a positive and motivating environment. Regularly revisiting and celebrating the network's mission and vision can remind members of the larger purpose behind their efforts, reinforcing their commitment.

In addition to these strategies, leveraging technology can play a significant role in keeping activists connected and motivated. Online collaboration tools and platforms can facilitate seamless communication, coordination, and resource-sharing. Virtual events, discussion forums, and social media groups can provide spaces for ongoing interaction, even when physical meetings are not possible. Utilizing multimedia content such as videos, podcasts, and infographics can make learning and engagement more dynamic and accessible.

Measuring and Celebrating Success

Tracking progress and celebrating milestones are crucial components in building effective activist networks. These practices not only reinforce commitment but also maintain the momentum necessary to drive collective impact. Activists need tangible evidence of their progress to stay motivated and feel a sense of accomplishment. By highlighting achievements and recognizing the efforts of individuals within the network, activists can stay engaged and continue to work toward their goals with renewed energy.

Setting measurable goals is the cornerstone of tracking progress. Without clear objectives, it is challenging to gauge the effectiveness of any activism effort. Measurable goals provide direction and focus, allowing activists to concentrate their efforts on specific targets. For instance, an environmental activist group might set a goal to reduce plastic waste in their community by 50% within a year. This goal is specific, time-bound, and measurable, providing a clear benchmark against which progress can be assessed.

In addition to setting goals, it is essential to use metrics effectively. Data and analytics play a vital role in monitoring activities and outcomes. By collecting and analyzing relevant data, activists can track their progress accurately and make informed decisions about how to adjust their strategies. For example, if the same environmental group notices that their waste reduction efforts are not yielding the expected results, they can use data to identify what isn't working and pivot their approach accordingly. Metrics offer objective insights that help fine-tune actions to maximize impact.

Publicizing achievements is another powerful tool for reinforcing commitment and building momentum. When successes are shared with the broader community, it not only celebrates the hard work of those involved but also attracts additional support. Public recognition can come in various forms, such as social media posts, press releases, or community events. By spreading the word about accomplishments, activists can draw attention to their cause and inspire others to join their efforts. For instance, sharing the story of a successful clean-up campaign can motivate other communities to undertake similar initiatives, amplifying the overall impact.

Organizing celebration events to mark significant milestones is a practical way to recognize collective effort and reinforce shared purpose. These events serve multiple purposes: they provide a platform to reflect on what has been achieved, thank everyone who contributed, and plan the next steps. A well-organized celebration can range from a simple gathering to a full-scale event with guest speakers, entertainment, and awards. For example, an activist network focused on educational reforms might hold an annual gala to celebrate progress made in increasing school funding or improving graduation rates. Such events acknowledge the hard work of participants and foster a sense of unity and motivation.

Celebrating milestones and tracking progress can enhance the cohesion and resilience of activist networks. Recognizing small wins along the way is just as important as celebrating major achievements. Small victories provide frequent opportunities to boost morale and remind everyone involved that their efforts are making a difference. Whether it's successfully organizing a local protest or gaining new followers on social media, each achievement contributes to the larger goal and deserves acknowledgment.

Moreover, activating a culture of celebration within the network encourages continuous engagement and participation. It helps build a supportive environment where members feel valued and appreciated. Regularly acknowledging contributions, whether through formal events or informal shout-outs, fosters a positive and inclusive atmosphere. For instance, a youth-led climate action group could have monthly meet-ups where they highlight individual contributions, share stories of recent successes, and discuss future plans. This practice not only strengthens relationships within the group but also keeps the spirit of activism alive.

Creating a structured process for tracking progress and celebrating milestones can sustain long-term engagement. Implementing tools and practices to regularly monitor goals, gather feedback, and celebrate achievements ensures ongoing motivation and alignment with the network's purpose. Digital platforms like project management tools can assist in tracking tasks and milestones, while social media and email newsletters can be used to share updates and celebrate successes widely. For instance, a digital dashboard displaying key metrics and milestones can be a constant visual reminder of progress, keeping everyone focused and motivated.

Ultimately, the act of tracking and celebrating serves to deepen the connection between members and their cause. It reinforces the understanding that every effort, no matter how small, contributes to the overarching mission. As members witness the tangible results of their work, their belief in the possibility of change is strengthened, driving them to persist in their efforts despite challenges. This sustained engagement is critical for the growth and success of activist networks.

Insights and Implications

In this chapter, we explored various strategies for creating and maintaining strong activist networks. We discussed the importance of recruiting like-minded individuals by identifying and communicating core values that unify the cause. Additionally, we highlighted the need for diverse outreach methods, such as community events and social media, to attract a wide range of supporters. The significance of engagement through events, follow-up, and inclusion was also emphasized to ensure that new recruits remain active and valued within the network.

We also examined effective communication within networks, detailing the importance of clear protocols, collaboration tools, open feedback, and compelling updates. Utilizing digital platforms for expansion was another key focus, with insights on building a robust online presence and leveraging social media for engagement. Lastly, we stressed the importance of sustaining long-term engagement by recognizing contributions, providing continuing education, and fostering a supportive community. By employing these strategies, activists can build cohesive networks that drive impactful social change.

CHAPTER 3

Navigating the Legislative Maze

N avigating the legislative maze is a task that requires both knowledge and strategy. Understanding how legislation works and how to influence it can seem daunting, but breaking down the process into manageable steps makes it accessible. Whether you're tracking bills, engaging with key decision-makers, or assessing the impact of proposed laws, each part of the process plays a vital role in effective legislative advocacy.

In this chapter, you will learn about the various tools available for tracking legislative developments in real-time and how to set up alerts to stay informed without being overwhelmed. We will explore the intricacies of committee processes, including the different types of committees and their roles in shaping legislation. You'll also discover how to analyze bill summaries to understand their implications for various communities and learn techniques for evaluating the potential social, economic, and environmental impacts of proposed laws. Finally, we will discuss strategies for identifying and engaging key decision-makers, creating engagement plans, and leveraging public opinion to amplify your advocacy efforts. By mastering these skills, you will be well-equipped to navigate the legislative landscape and make meaningful contributions to the causes you care about.

Tracking Legislation and Understanding Its Impact

Navigating the legislative maze requires a solid understanding of how to track legislative developments and assess their implications. Here's how you can equip yourself with these essential skills.

Using Legislative Tracking Tools

In today's digital age, various online platforms make it easier than ever to monitor legislation in real-time. These tools help you stay informed about new bills, amendments, and other significant changes as they happen. Some popular examples include GovTrack, LegiScan, and OpenCongress. Each platform offers unique features. For instance, GovTrack allows users to follow specific bills and receive notifications about updates, while LegiScan provides comprehensive state-level tracking.

Understanding how to set up alerts for bills that matter to your cause is crucial. Most tracking tools have alert systems where you can choose to receive email or text notifications about particular legislative actions. By customizing these alerts, you ensure that you're always in the loop without being overwhelmed by irrelevant information.

Learning the importance of timeline tracking to stay informed on key legislative deadlines is another critical aspect. Many tracking tools come equipped with calendars that highlight important dates, such as committee hearings, voting sessions, and deadlines for amendments. By keeping an eye on these timelines, activists can plan their strategies effectively, ensuring they exert influence at the most impactful times.

Recognizing how to evaluate the importance of specific bills based on their positional effectiveness is equally vital. Not all bills are created equal; some have a higher chance of passing due to bipartisan support or backing from influential lawmakers. Tools like BillTrack50 provide analysis and scoring systems that help you gauge the likelihood of a bill's success. This allows activists to prioritize their efforts and focus on supporting legislation with the best chances of making a positive impact.

Understanding Committee Processes

Committees play a pivotal role in shaping legislation. Every bill must pass through one or more committees before it reaches the entire legislative body for a vote. Understanding the committee system is crucial because it affects the trajectory of proposed laws. Committees conduct detailed examinations of bills, hold hearings, and make amendments. They serve as the initial gatekeepers, determining whether a bill will proceed or stall.

There are different types of committees, including standing committees, select committees, and joint committees. Standing committees are permanent and handle ongoing issues, whereas select committees are temporary and focused on specific inquiries. Joint committees consist of members from both legislative houses and usually tackle routine matters.

To influence the legislative process effectively, it's important to know which committee is handling the bill you care about. Often, committee chairs wield considerable influence, and reaching out to these key figures can amplify your advocacy efforts. Attending public hearings and participating in committee discussions can also provide valuable insights and opportunities to voice your opinions.

Analyzing Bill Summaries

Bill summaries condense complex legislative texts into more digestible formats. Learning to read and interpret these summaries is an essential skill for any activist. Bill summaries often outline the purpose, key provisions, and potential impacts of proposed legislation. They simplify dense legal language, making it easier for the general public to understand what's at stake.

Start by identifying the bill's main objectives. Look for sections that describe the problem the bill aims to address and the proposed solutions. Pay attention to any financial implications, such as funding requirements or budget reallocations. These sections are crucial because they reveal the practical feasibility of the bill.

Another important aspect is to distinguish between mandatory provisions and discretionary guidelines. Mandatory provisions are those that must be followed if the bill passes, while discretionary guidelines offer suggestions or recommendations. Knowing the difference helps you evaluate the bill's enforceability and potential impact.

Additionally, bill summaries often include statements of intent from the bill's sponsors. These statements provide context and insight into the motivations behind the legislation, helping you understand its broader goals. Comparing multiple bill summaries can also shed light on differing approaches to similar issues, aiding in the development of well-rounded advocacy strategies.

Assessing the Impact of Legislation

Evaluating how proposed laws affect local communities is a critical part of legislative activism. Frameworks for assessing the impact of legislation involve several key steps. First, identify the stakeholders affected by the bill. Stakeholders can include different community groups, businesses, government agencies, and non-profits. Understanding who stands to gain or lose from the legislation helps in crafting targeted advocacy messages.

Next, analyze the potential social, economic, and environmental impacts of the bill. Social impacts might include changes in public services, education, or healthcare. Economic impacts could involve job creation, tax changes, or shifts in market dynamics. Environmental impacts might relate to resource use, pollution levels, or conservation efforts. Using tools like cost-benefit analysis can provide a more quantified understanding of these impacts.

Engaging with community members is another essential step in assessing legislative impacts. Conduct surveys, host town hall meetings, and participate in forums to gather firsthand accounts of how proposed laws might affect people's lives. This grassroots feedback is invaluable for informed activism and can be used to persuade lawmakers by presenting real-world implications.

Finally, consider the longer-term consequences of the legislation. Some laws may have immediate benefits but cause adverse effects down the line. Others may require initial sacrifices for future gains. A thorough assessment involves looking beyond the surface to anticipate and mitigate possible unintended consequences.

Identifying and Engaging Key Decision-Makers

One of the key aspects of effective advocacy is knowing how to find and connect with the individuals who hold the power to influence policy decisions. This subpoint will guide you through the essential steps and strategies to identify, understand, and engage with elected officials and other decision-makers.

Researching Elected Officials

The first step in successful advocacy work is identifying the right officials to engage with. Start by determining which level of government—local, state, or federal—is responsible for the policy area you are concerned about. Each level of government has specific roles and responsibilities. Understanding these can help you target your efforts more effectively.

To research elected officials, use reliable sources like official government websites, which often list contact information and committee assignments. Tools like Project Vote Smart and OpenSecrets.org can provide in-depth profiles on politicians, including their voting records, campaign contributions, and top issues. Social media platforms can also offer insights into what issues are currently important to them.

Once you have identified key officials, look into their backgrounds. Knowing their professional history, political affiliations, and public statements can give you a better understanding of their priorities and potential openness to your advocacy work. Pay particular attention to committees they serve on, as these are often influential in legislative processes related to specific issues.

Mapping the Power Structure

After identifying who to engage, the next step is mapping the power structure. Visualizing relationships between decision-makers and the legislative process can help you see where influence can be most effectively applied. Begin by creating a diagram that illustrates the connections between key players within the legislative body. Include elected officials, committee members, and other influential figures such as lobbyists, advisors, and advocacy groups.

Use this map to identify allies and opponents among decision-makers. Understanding these dynamics will allow you to craft more targeted and effective strategies. For example, if you notice that a particular official has a strong alliance with another influential leader, engaging both simultaneously may amplify your message.

Additionally, consider the role of informal networks and behind-the-scenes influencers. Legislative staffers, policy advisors, and even influential constituents can play significant roles in shaping lawmakers' opinions and actions. Identifying and engaging with these individuals can provide additional pathways for influence.

Creating a Plan for Engagement

With your research and power mapping complete, the next step is creating a plan for engagement. Start by setting clear objectives for what you want to achieve through your interactions with decision-makers. Whether it's scheduling a meeting, getting a commitment of support, or simply initiating a dialogue, having defined goals will guide your approach and help measure success.

Next, tailor your communication strategy to each official based on your research. Personalize your messages to address their interests and concerns directly. Crafting compelling narratives that resonate personally with the official can make your advocacy more persuasive. Employ various methods of communication, including letters, emails, phone calls, and social media outreach. Each medium has its own strengths, so using a combination can maximize your reach and impact.

Another crucial aspect of your plan should involve building coalitions. Working with other advocacy groups or organizations that share your goals can strengthen your position. Collaborate to organize events, sign petitions, and raise awareness collectively; demonstrating broad public support can significantly bolster your cause.

When planning in-person meetings or calls, ensure you come prepared with clear, concise, and evidence-backed talking points. Practice these beforehand to ensure you deliver your message confidently and effectively. Also, be ready to answer questions or provide additional information upon request.

Leveraging Public Opinion

Public opinion plays a powerful role in influencing policymakers. Understanding how to mobilize citizen advocates can amplify your efforts and create a groundswell of support that decision-makers cannot easily ignore. Start by educating the public about the issue at hand. Use accessible language and relatable examples to explain why it matters and what is at stake.

Social media campaigns, blog posts, and community meetings are effective ways to spread your message. Encourage people to engage by sharing content, signing petitions, and contacting their representatives. Grassroots movements can build momentum quickly, especially when harnessed through modern communication tools.

Organize public demonstrations or town hall meetings to bring visibility to your cause. Invite the media to cover these events to reach a broader audience. Stories that highlight personal experiences related to the issue can be particularly compelling. Media coverage not only raises public awareness but also puts additional pressure on decision-makers.

Engage influencers and thought leaders who can lend credibility and broaden the reach of your advocacy efforts. These individuals can help frame your issue in a way that resonates with diverse audiences. Additionally, utilizing data and statistics in your messaging can enhance your argument and demonstrate the broad support for your stance.

Techniques for Lobbying and Advocacy

Understanding lobbying regulations is crucial for anyone looking to advance their causes within the legislative arena. Lobbying is an essential tool in advocacy, but it is governed by a host of rules and regulations designed to ensure transparency and fairness. Each jurisdiction has its own set of laws that define what is permissible behavior for lobbyists. For instance, federal law in the United States requires lobbyists to register and report their activities, including any expenditures made to influence legislation. Understanding these legal frameworks can help you avoid potential pitfalls and ensure your efforts remain above board.

Beyond understanding these regulations, crafting a compelling lobbying message is perhaps the most critical aspect of effective lobbying. A well-developed narrative can capture the attention of lawmakers and make your cause more relatable and urgent. To craft a convincing message, start by identifying the core values and concerns that resonate with the legislators you aim to influence.

Research their previous voting records, speeches, and public statements to tailor your message in a way that aligns with their interests and priorities.

A strong lobbying message often includes personal stories or examples that highlight the real-world impact of the issue at hand. Data and statistics can bolster these narratives by providing credible evidence to support your claims. However, it is important to strike a balance between emotional appeal and factual integrity. Legislators are more likely to be swayed by arguments that are both heartfelt and grounded in reality.

In addition to crafting compelling messages, utilizing lobbying days and events can create invaluable opportunities for face-to-face advocacy with decision-makers. These events provide a platform to meet with legislators, their staff, and other key stakeholders in a more informal setting. Lobbying days, often organized by advocacy groups, allow participants to come together and present a unified front on specific issues. By participating in these events, you can amplify the voice of your cause and increase the chances of your message being heard.

When attending lobbying events, preparation is key. Make sure to rehearse your talking points and practice answering potential questions. Bring along briefing materials, such as fact sheets and policy briefs, to leave behind with legislators. These documents can serve as useful references long after the meeting is over. Additionally, following up with a thank-you note or email can reinforce your commitment and keep the lines of communication open.

Building alliances with other organizations is another vital strategy for strengthening the impact of your lobbying efforts. Collaborating with like-minded groups can enhance your credibility and demonstrate broad-based support for your cause. Alliances can take many forms, from informal networks to formal coalitions, each offering unique advantages. Partnering with established organizations can lend legitimacy to your efforts, while grassroots groups can bring energy and local knowledge to the table.

To successfully build alliances, start by identifying organizations whose missions align with yours. Reach out to them to discuss potential collaboration opportunities and explore ways to combine resources and expertise. Joint initiatives, co-hosted events, and coordinated advocacy campaigns are just a few examples of how organizations can work together to achieve common goals. By pooling your strengths and sharing your insights, you can create a more powerful and effective lobbying force.

Moreover, regular communication and transparency are essential to maintaining strong alliances. Keep your partners informed about your activities and progress, and be open to feedback and suggestions. Trust and mutual respect are the foundations of any successful collaboration, so invest time in building and nurturing these relationships.

To summarize, navigating the legislative maze effectively requires a thorough understanding of lobbying regulations, the ability to craft compelling messages, strategic participation in lobbying days and events, and the formation of strong alliances with other organizations. By mastering these techniques, you can significantly enhance your ability to influence legislation and advance your causes within the legislative arena.

Analyzing Bill Summaries and Implications

Analyzing and interpreting bill summaries is a crucial skill for anyone involved in advocacy or civic activities. Bill summaries distill complex legislative language into more understandable text, providing insights into the potential impacts on various populations. Understanding how to effectively read these summaries can help you gauge implications and craft informed advocacy strategies.

The first step in analyzing a bill summary is learning to distinguish key passages that highlight the potential impact on specific populations. Key passages often provide clues about who will be most affected by the proposed legislation. For instance, a bill concerning healthcare reform may include sections detailing changes to Medicaid or Medicare, which primarily affect low-income individuals and the elderly. By identifying such passages, you can better understand how different demographics might be impacted.

When distinguishing these key passages, focus on language that mentions specific groups or sectors. Look for terms like "low-income families," "small businesses," "veterans," or "students." These identifiers can guide you in assessing which segments of the population will feel the ramifications of the legislation most acutely. Understanding these details allows you to frame your analysis around the real-world implications for those communities.

Another critical aspect is distinguishing pros and cons during the analysis stage. Every piece of legislation comes with potential benefits and drawbacks. Being able to identify these can inform your advocacy strategies and help you communicate effectively with stakeholders. For example, while a new tax policy might reduce rates for middle-class families, it could also lead to cuts in public services. Weighing these pros and cons ensures that your arguments are balanced and well-informed.

During your analysis, create a list of positive impacts alongside negative ones. This methodical approach helps clarify where you stand on the issue and prepares you to engage in constructive debates. It is also essential for crafting compelling messages that resonate with lawmakers and the public. Acknowledge the bill's advantages while also pointing out its shortcomings to present a more nuanced perspective.

Using bill summaries to communicate the complexities of legislation to broader audiences is another key component. Many people find legislative language confusing and inaccessible. Your role as an advocate is to bridge that gap. Simplify the bill's provisions without losing the essence of what it aims to accomplish. By doing so, you make it easier for others to understand and get involved in the advocacy process.

To communicate effectively, break down the bill into digestible sections. Use plain language and avoid jargon. For instance, if you're explaining a bill that proposes changes in environmental regulations, articulate what those changes mean for local communities, businesses, and natural habitats. Use analogies and real-life examples to illustrate your points clearly. This approach will help demystify the legislative process and encourage more people to participate in civic engagement.

Identifying critical data points to support arguments during advocacy efforts is immensely valuable. Data lends credibility to your arguments and can sway opinions by showcasing tangible evidence. When reading a bill summary, look for statistics, dates, case studies, and expert testimonials that back up your points. These elements can be powerful tools in persuading both lawmakers and the general public.

For example, if advocating for an education bill, support your stance with data showing improved graduation rates in districts with similar policies. Cite reputable sources and ensure that your data is current and relevant. Including such data points makes your arguments more persuasive and authoritative, enhancing the likelihood of achieving your advocacy goals.

In practice, let's consider a hypothetical bill focused on climate change mitigation. To analyze this bill, start by pinpointing key passages that discuss its impact on specific populations. Look for sections detailing measures like subsidies for renewable energy companies or penalties for industries with high carbon emissions. This information will help you identify who stands to benefit or lose from the legislation.

Next, weigh the pros and cons. The bill might offer significant environmental benefits by reducing carbon footprints, but it could also impose financial burdens on certain industries. Highlight these aspects in your analysis to provide a balanced view. Share this information through platforms accessible to your audience, whether it's social media, community meetings, or informational brochures.

Communicate the bill's complexities by breaking down its main components. Explain how subsidies will incentivize clean energy adoption and how penalties aim to reduce pollution. Use straightforward language and concrete examples to make these concepts relatable. For instance, compare the environmental benefits seen in countries with similar policies to show potential outcomes.

Lastly, bolster your advocacy with critical data points. Gather statistics on the success of comparable programs elsewhere and expert opinions supporting the bill's effectiveness. Present these findings in your discussions and written materials to fortify your arguments.

Utilizing Legislative Tracking Tools Effectively

Staying informed and proactive in legislative advocacy can be daunting, but using legislative tracking tools can make the process more manageable. These tools offer a strategic way to monitor legislative developments and ensure you're always in the loop about bills relevant to your cause.

First and foremost, setting up alerts for bills that matter to your advocacy efforts is crucial. Many online platforms allow you to create personalized alerts that notify you when there is movement on specific legislation. This feature ensures you receive timely updates and don't miss critical actions such as committee hearings or votes. For instance, if you are advocating for environmental protections, you can set up an alert for any new bills addressing climate change. Receiving these notifications directly in your email or through an app allows you to respond promptly, whether it's rallying support from your community or contacting lawmakers.

Another essential aspect of legislative tracking is understanding and utilizing timeline tracking. Legislative processes follow a strict calendar with key deadlines for bill submissions, committee evaluations, amendments, and voting sessions. Keeping track of these timelines is vital so you know when to act. Missing a deadline can mean missing an opportunity to influence the outcome. By syncing legislative timelines with your own calendar, you can plan your advocacy activities around these critical dates. For example, knowing when a public hearing is scheduled gives you ample time to organize testimonies or gather community support.

The importance of recognizing the value of different online platforms for monitoring legislative actions cannot be overstated. Numerous websites and apps are available that provide real-time updates on legislative activities. Platforms such as govtrack.us, Congress.gov, and state-specific sites like California's LegInfo offer comprehensive databases where you can track bills, understand their status, and see who supports or opposes them. These tools often include features like bill summaries, voting records, and legislator contact information, making it easier for you to stay informed and take action. Using multiple platforms can also provide cross-referenced information, ensuring you have a well-rounded view of the legislative landscape.

Legislative tracking tools are not just beneficial for following the progress of legislation; they also enhance community surveys and data collection. These tools can help identify trends and gather quantitative data that strengthens your advocacy. For instance, if you're working on education reform, you can use tracking tools to analyze how similar bills have fared in other states, what arguments were made in their favor or against them, and gather statistical evidence to support your case. This data can be invaluable when presenting your arguments to legislators or during public campaigns. Moreover, sharing this information with your community can galvanize support and increase involvement in advocacy efforts.

Understanding how to effectively use these tools involves some initial learning but pays off significantly in the long run. Start by familiarizing yourself with the basic functions of each platform. Tutorials, webinars, and help sections provided by these sites can be very useful. Once comfortable, move on to exploring advanced features like bill comparison tools, trend analysis, and constituency mapping. These features can provide deeper insights into the legislative process and reveal opportunities for more strategic advocacy.

Collaborating with others in your community who are also using these tools can further enhance your advocacy. Sharing alerts, pooling resources, and strategizing together can lead to more coordinated and effective efforts. Community meetings to discuss upcoming legislative actions, potential impacts, and planned responses can be instrumental. This collaborative approach ensures that everyone is on the same page and can act swiftly and cohesively.

Additionally, integrating legislative tracking tools with social media and communication channels can amplify your advocacy efforts. Sharing real-time updates, urgent calls to action, and informational posts about legislative developments can engage a broader audience. Tools like Twitter, Facebook, and Instagram can be powerful platforms for raising awareness and mobilizing supporters quickly. Encourage your followers to set up their own alerts and share information within their networks. This ripple effect can exponentially increase the reach and impact of your advocacy.

Moreover, consider organizing workshops or training sessions to teach others how to use these legislative tracking tools. Providing hands-on experience and practical tips can empower more people to get involved. Tailor these sessions to different skill levels, ensuring that both beginners and more experienced users find value. Utilize local libraries, community centers, or virtual meeting spaces to conduct these trainings, making them accessible to a wide audience.

Lastly, continually evaluate and adjust your use of legislative tracking tools. Advocacy is a dynamic field, and being flexible and adaptable is crucial. Regularly review the effectiveness of your alerts, the platforms you are using, and your overall strategy. Gather feedback from your community and incorporate it into your approach. Staying updated with new features or better tools available in the market can provide additional advantages.

Closing Remarks

Understanding and influencing the legislative process is a vital skill for anyone involved in advocacy. This chapter has provided you with essential tools and strategies to navigate this complex landscape. By familiarizing yourself with legislative tracking tools, you can stay informed about new bills and critical deadlines, allowing you to act swiftly and effectively. Recognizing the role of committees and how they shape legislation highlights the importance of engaging with key decision-makers at the right stages. Additionally, learning to analyze bill summaries helps you grasp the potential impacts on various stakeholders, enabling you to craft more persuasive arguments.

Effective advocacy also involves identifying and connecting with influential figures who shape policy decisions. Through detailed research and strategic planning, you can tailor your communication to resonate with elected officials and other decision-makers. Leveraging public opinion and building alliances further strengthens your position, creating a unified front that amplifies your cause. By mastering these techniques, you can enhance your ability to influence legislation and contribute meaningfully to social change.

As you move forward, continue to apply these principles, staying proactive and engaged in the legislative process.

CHAPTER 4

Media Mastery for Activists

Mastering the use of media is a crucial skill for activists aiming to shape public opinion and drive change. This chapter provides a comprehensive guide on how to effectively leverage various media platforms to amplify activist causes. Understanding how to craft compelling messages, engaging narratives, and powerful visuals is fundamental to capturing attention and inspiring action. By tailoring these elements to resonate with different audiences, activists can significantly enhance their impact and broaden their reach.

Throughout this chapter, you will learn practical strategies for creating persuasive messages that connect with your audience on an emotional level. The discussion covers the importance of understanding your audience's values, interests, and concerns to tailor messages accordingly. Additionally, the chapter delves into the art of developing clear and engaging narratives, supported by real-life testimonials and strong visuals like infographics, which simplify complex data. You will also discover effective ways to create calls to action that prompt immediate engagement, as well as tips for balancing traditional and new media to maximize reach. Finally, the chapter explores the significance of maintaining relationships with journalists and using social media to engage directly with supporters, ensuring your cause remains visible and influential in today's fast-paced information landscape.

Crafting Compelling Messages and Narratives

To create persuasive messages that resonate with an audience and further activist causes, it is crucial to start by understanding your audience. Knowing who you are speaking to helps tailor the message to align with their values, interests, and concerns. For example, if your audience consists primarily of university students passionate about environmental issues, emphasizing the impact of climate change on future job prospects could be a powerful angle. This shows them how the issue directly affects their lives and motivates them to engage more deeply.

Developing a clear narrative is essential for keeping your audience engaged. A well-structured story that includes a beginning, middle, and end can be very compelling. Incorporating testimonials within this narrative adds authenticity and credibility. Real-life stories from individuals who have been affected by the issue can make abstract concepts more relatable and emotional. For instance, if you are advocating for mental health awareness, sharing personal experiences from people who have overcome challenges can provide inspiration and a sense of connection.

Strong visuals are another key component in creating persuasive messages. Utilizing infographics can help simplify complex data, making it easier for your audience to understand. Visual aids can break down statistics into bite-sized pieces of information that are more digestible. For example, an infographic showing the increase in plastic pollution over the years can highlight the urgency of adopting sustainable practices. By presenting data visually, you facilitate quicker comprehension and retention of the information.

Creating a call to action is vital for prompting immediate engagement. Being specific in your requests increases the likelihood that your audience will take the desired action. Instead of a vague plea like "Get involved," a more precise request such as "Sign our petition to ban single-use plastics in our city" provides clear guidance on what steps they need to take. This specificity reduces ambiguity and makes it easier for people to follow through with their intentions.

Understanding your audience goes beyond basic demographics; it involves diving into their psychographics—their attitudes, aspirations, and other psychological criteria. Tailoring the language and tone of your message based on these insights can significantly improve receptivity. If your target audience values straightforward and factual communication, adopting a direct tone with ample evidence will likely resonate more. Conversely, if they appreciate narratives rich in empathy and emotion, a more heartfelt approach may be effective.

When developing your narrative, it is important to maintain coherence and relevance to the central issue. Each part of the story should contribute to the overarching message you want to convey. Avoid adding extraneous details that could divert attention away from your main point. To illustrate, if your goal is to advocate for education reform, stick to stories and examples directly related to educational challenges and solutions, rather than veering into unrelated areas.

Visuals should complement and enhance your narrative, not overshadow it. While striking images and graphics can capture attention, they should always tie back to your core message. An effective approach is to use visuals that evoke the right emotions or highlight key facts. For activism around homelessness, for instance, photos of local shelters and infographics showing the benefits of housing programs can provide compelling visual support to your narrative.

Calls to action should be strategically integrated throughout your message, not just at the end. Repeatedly nudging your audience towards taking a specific action can reinforce the importance and urgency of the task. However, each call to action should feel natural within the context of the message, avoiding any semblance of forcefulness or coercion.

Engaging with Traditional and New Media

Recognizing the Role of Traditional Media

Traditional media continues to play a significant role in shaping public opinion. Establishing relationships with journalists is crucial for activists who want to ensure their messages are heard. Journalists have access to large audiences and can amplify your cause, providing legitimacy and reach that might be more challenging to achieve through other means.

To build these relationships, start by identifying journalists who cover topics related to your activism. Reach out with an introduction and explain why your cause is important. Be concise but impactful. It's beneficial to offer them exclusive stories or insights that will intrigue their audience. Over time, consistent communication and collaboration can lead to more favorable coverage. Remember, journalists are often swamped with pitches, so making yours stand out is essential.

Maintaining this relationship involves being reliable and responsive. When a journalist contacts you for a comment or interview, respond promptly. Providing timely and accurate information builds trust and positions you as a credible source. Attending local media events and press conferences can also facilitate face-to-face interactions, further strengthening these connections.

Utilizing New Media

New media platforms like social media, blogs, and podcasts offer activists unique opportunities to engage with audiences directly. One key strategy is consistent posting. Regular updates keep your audience informed and engaged, ensuring that your cause remains visible amidst the constant influx of information online.

Creating content consistently does not mean sacrificing quality. It's essential to understand your audience and what type of content resonates with them. Whether it's educational posts, behind-the-scenes looks at your activities, or interactive Q&A sessions, maintaining a steady flow of diverse content can help keep your audience interested and invested.

In addition to regular posting, engaging directly with your followers is vital. Respond to comments, ask for feedback, and create opportunities for conversation. This two-way communication fosters a sense of community and makes your supporters feel valued. Many successful movements have leveraged hashtags to create a broader sense of solidarity and make their cause trending topics on social media.

Balancing Different Media Types

Effectively balancing traditional and new media types can significantly enhance the reach and impact of your message. Cross-promotion is one way to maximize message reach across different platforms. For example, if you have an upcoming event, promote it via a press release to traditional media outlets while simultaneously creating social media posts to generate buzz among your followers.

Using a variety of media formats – such as articles, videos, infographics, and podcasts – caters to different preferences within your audience. Some people may prefer reading an in-depth article, while others might engage better with a short video or podcast episode. By diversifying your content, you cater to various learning and engagement styles, which can broaden your overall reach.

A practical approach to cross-promotion involves repurposing content. A compelling story shared during an interview with a local newspaper can be adapted into a blog post or a series of tweets. Visuals from a campaign can be used in both print materials and digital platforms. This method ensures that your message remains consistent across channels while tapped into the strengths of each medium.

Measuring Media Engagement

Monitoring how the public responds to your media efforts is pivotal in guiding future messaging. Tools like Google Analytics, social media insights, and media monitoring services can provide valuable data on how your content is performing. These metrics can include reach, impressions, engagement rates, and more.

For social media, focus on likes, shares, comments, and follower growth. High engagement rates typically indicate that your content resonates well with your audience. On traditional media fronts, monitor mentions in news articles, television segments, or radio shows. You can gauge your campaign's success by analyzing the tone and frequency of these mentions.

Understanding these metrics allows you to identify what works and what doesn't, enabling adjustments to improve your strategy over time. For instance, if particular types of posts receive more engagement, consider creating similar content more frequently. Conversely, if some messages don't resonate, analyze why they fell flat and adjust accordingly.

Additionally, soliciting direct feedback from your audience can offer qualitative insights that numbers alone can't provide. Conduct surveys or polls to gather opinions on your campaigns and suggestions for improvement. This feedback loop helps refine your approach and creates a sense of involvement among your supporters.

Developing a Clear Narrative

Crafting a clear and compelling narrative is essential for any activist movement. A strong narrative can make abstract issues personal and relatable, leading to greater public support and understanding. Begin by identifying the core message of your campaign and distilling it into a simple, memorable statement. This "elevator pitch" should capture the essence of your cause in a way that's easy to understand and repeat.

Your narrative should include real-life stories and testimonials to humanize the issue. These personal accounts add authenticity and can evoke emotional responses, making your message more powerful. Highlighting the experiences of those directly affected by the issue brings the cause closer to people's hearts and minds.

Using conflict and resolution frameworks can enhance drama and urgency in your storytelling. Presenting a problem and then showing how your movement aims to solve it can galvanize support and action. Demonstrating the tangible impacts of your efforts and outlining clear calls to action encourages people to get involved.

Managing Social Media Campaigns Effectively

Setting Clear Objectives

The first step in organizing and executing a successful social media campaign is setting clear objectives. Without a well-defined goal, it's easy for your efforts to become scattered and ineffective. The SMART criteria—Specific, Measurable, Achievable, Relevant, and Time-bound—provide a robust framework for ensuring that your objectives are both attainable and impactful.

To start, make sure your objectives are specific. Instead of aiming to "raise awareness about climate change," specify exactly what you want to achieve, such as "increase the number of followers on our climate action page by 20%." This clarity will help guide your actions and keep your team focused.

Measurability is just as crucial. You need to establish metrics that will allow you to gauge your progress. If your goal is to increase engagement, decide on concrete indicators like the number of shares, comments, or likes. For example, "gain 500 comments on our series of posts within two weeks" is a measurable objective that can be tracked over time.

Achievability is another essential component. While it's commendable to set ambitious goals, they also need to be realistic. Assess your resources, including time, manpower, and budget, before setting objectives. Unrealistic goals can demoralize your team and diminish the effectiveness of your campaign. Therefore, an achievable goal might look something like "secure 100 new followers this month based on current trends and resource allocation."

Your objectives should also be relevant to your overarching mission. Ask yourself whether achieving these goals will bring you closer to your ultimate aim. For instance, if your primary mission is to advocate for policy changes around renewable energy, then building a larger online community can serve as a powerful support mechanism for lobbying efforts.

Lastly, every objective must be time-bound. Set deadlines for each milestone to foster a sense of urgency and spur continuous progress. Phrasing your objective as "achieve a 15% increase in post engagement over the next three months" sets a clear timeframe, encouraging accountability among team members.

Developing a Content Strategy

Once your objectives are set, the next critical step is developing a content strategy that aligns with your goals. A well-thought-out content calendar ensures timely and relevant posts, helping to maintain engagement and drive your campaign forward.

Start by identifying the types of content that resonate with your target audience. Do they respond better to infographics, videos, or long-form articles? Conduct some initial research to understand their preferences and tailor your content accordingly. For example, young adults might engage more with visually appealing graphics and short, punchy videos, while community leaders may prefer in-depth articles and data-driven reports.

Plan your content calendar at least a month in advance. This will give you enough time to create high-quality material and ensure a steady flow of posts. Outline key dates and events that align with your cause, such as international awareness days, holidays, or related campaigns. For instance, if you're raising awareness about water conservation, you could plan a series of posts leading up to World Water Day.

Consistency is key in maintaining your audience's interest. Regularly scheduled posts can help build a loyal following and keep your cause top-of-mind. But consistency doesn't mean monotony; mix up your content to keep it interesting. Alternate between educational posts, personal stories, calls to action, and updates on your campaign's progress.

Engaging With Supporters

One crucial aspect of a successful social media campaign is engaging with your supporters. Active engagement strengthens community bonds and lends credibility to your cause.

Interactive sessions like live Q&As and forums offer excellent opportunities for real-time communication. Hosting a live Q&A session on Facebook or Instagram allows supporters to ask questions, voice concerns, and receive immediate responses. This direct interaction not only builds trust but also provides a platform for educating your audience on intricate aspects of your cause.

Forums, either on platforms like Reddit or specialized discussion boards, can sustain longer-term engagements. Here, participants can delve into more nuanced conversations, share experiences, and propose ideas. For example, if you're advocating for improved local public transport, a forum could be a space where users discuss existing issues, share success stories from other cities, and brainstorm potential solutions.

Beyond these interactive formats, regularly responding to comments and messages on your social media channels shows that you value your supporters' input. Acknowledging positive feedback, addressing criticisms constructively, and answering questions promptly can go a long way in fostering a genuine sense of community.

Analyzing Campaign Performance

No campaign is complete without analyzing its performance. Feedback loops are vital; they help you understand what worked, what didn't, and how you can improve future campaigns.

Start by collecting data from various analytics tools offered by social media platforms. Metrics like reach, engagement rate, click-through rate, and follower growth can provide valuable insights into your campaign's performance. For instance, if a particular post garnered significantly higher shares and comments, it indicates that the content resonated well with your audience.

Once you have gathered sufficient data, compare your results against the initial objectives you set. Did you meet your targets? If not, where did you fall short, and why might that be? This analysis will reveal patterns and highlight areas needing improvement. For example, if your goal was to increase engagement by 15% but only saw a 10% rise, scrutinize the types of posts that performed best and those that didn't.

Regularly scheduled reviews can help keep your campaign on track. Monthly assessments allow you to make real-time adjustments, ensuring that your strategy remains aligned with your objectives. During these reviews, involve your entire team to gather diverse perspectives and brainstorm new ideas.

Finally, consider conducting surveys or focus groups to get direct feedback from your audience. This qualitative data can offer deeper insights into your campaign's strengths and weaknesses. Simple questions like "What type of content do you find most useful?" or "How can we improve our engagement with you?" can produce actionable feedback.

Utilizing Visuals Effectively

In the realm of modern activism, understanding the role of strong visuals can significantly enhance the impact of your messages. Visuals not only capture attention but also evoke emotions, simplify complex information, and make issues more relatable to a broader audience. This subpoint will delve into several aspects that highlight the effectiveness of visuals in activism.

Emotional Impact

One of the most powerful ways visuals can enhance activist messages is by evoking emotions and reactions instantaneously. A well-chosen photograph or illustration can convey the urgency of an issue far more effectively than words alone. For instance, consider the iconic image of a polar bear stranded on a melting ice floe. This picture brings immediate awareness to the consequences of climate change without needing lengthy explanations. When people see such compelling images, they are more likely to feel moved, take action, and share the cause with others. These visual cues connect emotionally with viewers and can transform passive observers into active participants in your movement.

Simplifying Data

Infographics play a crucial role in turning complex data into easily understandable visuals. Activists often deal with statistics, survey results, and other forms of quantitative data that might be difficult for the general audience to grasp quickly. Infographics can distill this information into bite-sized, visually appealing pieces that are easier to digest and remember. For example, using a bar graph to illustrate income inequality across different demographics can make the data accessible and impactful. Simplified visuals help break down barriers to understanding and enable your audience to engage more critically and thoughtfully with your message.

High Shareability

In today's digital age, high shareability is key to spreading your message far and wide. Videos, in particular, capture attention and have high shareability on social media platforms. With the rise of short-form video content on apps like TikTok and Instagram Reels, activists have more opportunities than ever to create engaging, informative, and shareable content. A brief video explaining the significance of a protest or highlighting personal stories related to a cause can go viral, reaching thousands or even millions of people within minutes. This broadens your reach and brings new supporters to your cause, amplifying your efforts exponentially.

Visual Storytelling

Another essential aspect of using strong visuals in activism is visual storytelling. Using visual elements to build narratives makes issues more relatable and memorable. Humans are naturally drawn to stories, and a well-crafted visual narrative can draw people into your cause on a deeper level. For instance, creating a photo series that follows the daily life of a community affected by pollution tells a story that resonates more deeply than facts and figures alone. Visual storytelling allows you to present complex issues in a way that fosters empathy and understanding, bridging the gap between your message and your audience's emotions.

Building Relationships with Media Personnel

In today's fast-paced media environment, developing strong ties with media professionals is crucial for activists seeking consistent and favorable coverage. Forming these relationships can be the difference between a message that resonates widely and one that gets lost in the noise. Here, we will explore the significance of networking, pitching stories, crafting press releases, and following up with journalists.

Networking stands at the heart of building lasting relationships with media professionals. Attending media events such as press conferences, media summits, and industry mixers provides invaluable opportunities to meet journalists, editors, and producers face-to-face. These interactions allow activists to discuss their causes in a more personal manner, fostering genuine connections. Highlighting shared interests or values during these encounters can lay the groundwork for beneficial relationships. For instance, an activist advocating for environmental protection might connect with a journalist interested in climate change, paving the way for future collaboration.

Moreover, leveraging social media platforms like LinkedIn and Twitter can complement in-person networking efforts. Following and engaging with journalists online helps maintain visibility and demonstrates a vested interest in their work. A simple comment on a relevant article or a retweet can keep an activist on a journalist's radar, making it easier to reach out when pitching stories.

Knowing how to pitch stories effectively is another cornerstone of securing media coverage. A well-crafted pitch should be concise, compelling, and tailored to the recipient's interests and beats. Researching a journalist's previous work can provide insights into the types of stories they cover and their writing style. This information can be used to tailor the pitch, increasing its relevance and appeal.

When writing a pitch, it's essential to start with a compelling hook that grabs attention right away. This could be an interesting statistic, a powerful quote, or a thought-provoking question related to the cause. The body of the pitch should clearly state the activist's message, why it matters, and how it aligns with the journalist's audience. Including a call to action, such as suggesting an interview or providing additional resources, can also enhance the effectiveness of the pitch.

Press releases are another vital tool in an activist's media toolkit. An effective press release not only communicates key messages but also ensures they are presented in a clear and professional manner. Structuring the press release properly is paramount. It should include a headline that captures attention, a lead paragraph summarizing the main points, and subsequent paragraphs that provide more detailed information.

Writing in the inverted pyramid style—starting with the most important information and descending to less critical details—can help ensure that even if only a portion of the press release is read, the main message is conveyed. Additionally, including quotes from credible sources, such as experts or affected individuals, can add depth and authenticity to the narrative. Remember to end with contact information and any relevant links, guiding journalists on where to find further details or who to reach out to for interviews.

After sending out a pitch or press release, regular follow-ups are crucial to keeping journalists engaged. A polite follow-up email can serve as a gentle reminder and reiterate the importance of the story. Timing is key; wait a few days after the initial contact before following up to give the journalist time to consider the pitch. In the follow-up, briefly restate the main points of the original pitch or press release and express willingness to provide additional information or facilitate interviews.

Maintaining an ongoing dialogue beyond initial pitches can also foster stronger relationships. Periodically sharing updates about the cause or new developments can keep the story fresh in the journalist's mind. Even if a particular pitch doesn't get picked up, these continued interactions build familiarity and trust, increasing the likelihood of future coverage.

Personal touches in communication can also go a long way. Thanking journalists for previous coverage and acknowledging their work shows appreciation and respect, which can strengthen professional rapport. Celebrating small victories and milestones together, such as achieving project goals or receiving community support, can create a sense of shared accomplishment and solidarity.

Final Thoughts

Leveraging both traditional and new media is essential for activists aiming to shape public opinion and drive change. By understanding the audience and crafting compelling narratives, credible messages can be conveyed effectively. Strong visuals and clear calls to action further support these efforts by simplifying complex information and encouraging immediate engagement. Utilizing social media platforms enables direct communication with supporters, fostering a sense of community and making activism more accessible and impactful.

Building relationships with media personnel and measuring media engagement are crucial for sustaining long-term impact. Engaging consistently with journalists ensures broader reach and legitimacy, while constant evaluation helps refine strategies for better results. Activists can achieve meaningful progress by balancing various media types and focusing on clear objectives. This holistic approach ensures that the cause remains visible and relatable, inspiring others to join and take action.

CHAPTER 5

Policy AssessmentTools

E valuating local policies is an essential skill for anyone invested in their community's well-being. This chapter introduces interactive methods for assessing these policies, allowing readers to gain a deeper understanding of how specific initiatives impact their surroundings. By equipping themselves with these tools, individuals can make informed decisions and contribute more effectively to social activism and civic participation.

In this chapter, we will dive into four primary tools for policy assessment: Stakeholder Analysis, SWOT Analysis, Logic Models, and Cost-Benefit Analysis. Stakeholder Analysis helps identify everyone involved or affected by a policy, ensuring that diverse perspectives are considered. SWOT Analysis examines the strengths, weaknesses, opportunities, and threats associated with a policy, providing a comprehensive evaluation framework. Logic Models offer a visual representation of the resources required and the outcomes expected from a policy, mapping out the steps necessary for achieving goals. Finally, Cost-Benefit Analysis evaluates the economic impacts, comparing anticipated benefits against total costs to prioritize initiatives that maximize social good. Together, these methods provide a robust toolkit for analyzing and understanding the effectiveness of local policies.

Frameworks for Policy Analysis

Understanding how to analyze and evaluate local policies is crucial for any individual interested in social activism, community leadership, or civic participation. To achieve this, we must introduce essential frameworks that help readers critically assess the effectiveness of these policies. In this section, we will explore four key tools: Stakeholder Analysis, SWOT Analysis, Logic Models, and Cost-Benefit Analysis.

Stakeholder Analysis

Understanding various stakeholders involved in policy decisions is a fundamental aspect of evaluating local policies. Stakeholders include anyone who can affect or be affected by the policy. This group could range from government officials and business owners to community members and advocacy groups. Conducting a thorough stakeholder analysis enables us to identify vested interests and diverse perspectives. Recognizing these elements helps in understanding how different individuals or organizations might influence policy outcomes.

For instance, in a policy aimed at improving public transportation, stakeholders might include city planners, transportation companies, daily commuters, and environmental groups. Each of these stakeholders may have differing priorities and concerns. City planners may focus on infrastructure costs, transportation companies might be concerned about profitability, while daily commuters and environmental groups would be more interested in the affordability and eco-friendliness of the new system. By mapping out these interests, policymakers can create more inclusive and balanced policies.

Identifying power dynamics is another critical aspect of stakeholder analysis. Power dynamics often influence whose voices are heard and whose are sidelined. By acknowledging these dynamics, communities can advocate more effectively, striving for fair representation in policy discussions. For example, if business owners dominate the conversation around local economic development, the needs of low-income residents might be overshadowed. Recognizing this imbalance allows community leaders to push for more equitable involvement.

SWOT Analysis

SWOT (Strengths, Weaknesses, Opportunities, Threats) Analysis offers a structured approach to understanding the multifaceted impacts of policies. This tool encourages a comprehensive view, helping to pinpoint areas for improvement and potential innovations.

Consider a policy aimed at reducing homelessness. Strengths might include strong community support and available funding. Weaknesses could involve inadequate existing infrastructure or insufficient coordination among service providers. Opportunities might arise from potential partnerships with non-profits or federal grants. Threats might include political opposition or economic downturns that could strain resources.

By breaking down these elements, a SWOT Analysis highlights both internal and external factors that can affect a policy's success. It also emphasizes the importance of considering potential risks and benefits, ensuring that all aspects of a policy are thoroughly evaluated before implementation. This analytical method helps avoid unforeseen obstacles and maximizes the chances of achieving desired outcomes.

Logic Models

Logic models are visual tools used to map out the relationships between a policy's resources, activities, and expected outcomes. They provide clarity on how specific inputs translate into desired results. This model typically includes inputs (resources needed), activities (actions taken), outputs (direct products of activities), and outcomes (long-term impacts).

Let's take an educational policy aimed at improving student literacy rates. Inputs might include trained teachers, educational materials, and funding. Activities could involve teacher training workshops, curriculum development, and after-school reading programs. Outputs would be measurable things like the number of workshops held or books distributed. Outcomes would ideally be improved literacy rates among students.

Creating a logic model ensures that all stakeholders understand the steps required to achieve the policy goals and the resources needed at each stage. It facilitates communication and alignment among all parties involved, making it easier to track progress and make necessary adjustments. For instance, if after a year literacy rates haven't improved as expected, policymakers can look back at the model to identify whether there were issues in the inputs, activities, or outputs and adjust accordingly.

Cost-Benefit Analysis

Cost-benefit analysis (CBA) assesses the economic impacts of a policy by comparing its total expected costs against anticipated benefits. This method is crucial for driving the prioritization of initiatives that maximize overall social good. It emphasizes transparency in spending and resource allocation, ensuring that funds are utilized efficiently and effectively.

Imagine a policy proposed to build new parks in urban areas. Costs would include land acquisition, construction, maintenance, and staffing. Benefits might encompass increased property values, improved mental health of residents, and enhanced community cohesion. By quantifying these costs and benefits, CBA helps determine whether the park project is a worthwhile investment.

Moreover, CBA fosters accountability by providing a clear rationale for policy decisions. If a proposed policy shows more benefits than costs, it justifies the allocation of public funds towards that initiative. Conversely, if costs outweigh benefits, it signals the need to reconsider or modify the policy to enhance its efficiency. For example, if the initial plan for the parks reveals excessive construction costs, alternatives such as phased development or public-private partnerships might be explored to reduce financial burdens.

Using Data and Evidence in Assessments

In policy assessments, data-driven decision-making stands as a crucial component. This methodology empowers individuals to gather and interpret relevant data effectively, ensuring that decisions are based on solid evidence rather than mere intuition or speculation. By employing data-driven approaches, young adults, university students, community leaders, organizers, and previously disengaged citizens can make informed evaluations of policies impacting their communities.

Quantitative data collection forms the backbone of this approach. Collecting numerical data through surveys, demographic studies, and economic indicators provides an objective basis for evaluating policy impacts. For instance, surveys can reveal how many people in a community support a particular policy, while demographic studies might show which groups are most affected by it. Economic indicators, like employment rates or median income levels, can help assess whether a policy has had a positive or negative economic impact. This type of data is essential because it offers concrete proof of a policy's effectiveness, making it easier to advocate for necessary changes or improvements.

However, numbers alone cannot capture the full picture. Qualitative research methods play a complementary role in policy assessment. Techniques such as interviews and focus groups delve into the nuanced experiences of community members with specific policies. Through these methods, researchers can gather detailed narratives that highlight how policies affect people's daily lives, feelings, and perceptions. For example, while quantitative data might show that a new public transportation policy has increased bus usage, interviews with riders could uncover issues related to safety, convenience, or accessibility not apparent in the raw numbers. Engaging with community stories fosters empathy and ensures that diverse voices are heard and considered in the evaluation process.

Data visualization is another key element in making data-driven decision-making accessible and effective. Tools like charts, graphs, and infographics translate complex data into visually appealing and easily understandable formats. This method is particularly valuable for communicating findings to a broad audience, including policymakers, stakeholders, and the general public. For example, an infographic illustrating the benefits of a new environmental policy can quickly convey important information that might be overlooked in a dense report. By making data more digestible, visualization techniques enhance advocacy efforts and support transparent communication.

Publicly available data sources offer a treasure trove of information for policy assessment. Familiarity with local, state, and federal databases allows assessors to access necessary data without significant financial or logistical barriers. These sources often include datasets on health, education, economic performance, and more. For example, the U.S. Census Bureau provides comprehensive demographic information that can be invaluable for assessing community needs and policy impacts. Utilizing these resources fosters transparency and accountability in governance, as decisions are rooted in openly accessible data.

Employing these methods equips individuals with a robust toolkit for policy assessment. Quantitative data provides an empirical foundation, while qualitative research adds depth and context. Data visualization bridges the gap between complex data and diverse audiences, and publicly available data sources democratize access to critical information. Together, these tools empower readers to perform thorough, informed evaluations of local policies, fostering a more engaged and knowledgeable citizenry capable of driving positive change in their communities.

Gathering quantitative data requires meticulous planning and execution. Surveys must be designed to minimize bias and accurately reflect the population's opinions. Demographic studies should consider various factors such as age, gender, income, and ethnicity to ensure a comprehensive understanding of the community. Economic indicators need ongoing monitoring to capture trends over time. To achieve reliable results, it's crucial to employ sound statistical methods and seek input from experts in fields such as economics, sociology, and public health.

Qualitative research methods, while different in nature, also demand careful implementation. Conducting interviews involves crafting open-ended questions that encourage detailed responses and actively listening to participants' stories. Focus groups should be composed of diverse individuals to capture a wide range of perspectives. Analyzing qualitative data requires identifying common themes and patterns, which can then be integrated with quantitative findings to create a holistic view of policy impacts.

Data visualization is both an art and a science. Effective visualizations require selecting the right type of graphic for the data, whether it's bar charts for comparisons, line graphs for trends, or pie charts for proportions. Clarity and simplicity are paramount; cluttered graphics can confuse rather than inform. Color choices, labels, and annotations should be used thoughtfully to highlight key insights and guide viewers' interpretation of the data.

Leveraging publicly available data sources involves more than just accessing datasets; it requires understanding their scope, limitations, and appropriate applications. Not all data is created equal – some sources may be outdated, incomplete, or collected using different methodologies. Critical evaluation of data quality and relevance is essential. Additionally, combining data from multiple sources can provide a more comprehensive assessment but demands careful cross-referencing to ensure consistency and accuracy.

Equipped with these skills and tools, individuals can embark on informed policy assessments. For instance, a community leader evaluating a new housing policy might start by surveying residents to gather quantitative data on housing satisfaction and affordability. They could then conduct focus groups to explore personal experiences with housing conditions and identify specific challenges faced by different demographics. Visualizing this data through thoughtful charts and infographics can make a compelling case when presenting findings to local government officials. Additionally, referencing publicly available data on housing trends and economic conditions can bolster the assessment's credibility and comprehensiveness.

Case Studies of Successful Policy Evaluations – Local Level

Successful local policy evaluations can significantly impact community outcomes, providing valuable insights into the effectiveness of implemented policies. One notable example is the transformation in a mid-sized city that focused on improving public transportation. Initially plagued by unreliable service and limited routes, the city's policymakers embarked on a rigorous evaluation process to address these issues.

The evaluation began with extensive data collection through surveys and public consultations. Community members were asked about their primary concerns and suggestions for improvement. The policymakers then used this data to develop a comprehensive plan aimed at increasing route coverage and frequency while ensuring affordability and accessibility. The assessment included pilot programs, which allowed for real-time adjustments based on feedback and performance metrics. This iterative approach ensured that the community's needs were met dynamically, demonstrating the tangible benefits of thorough evaluations.

Analyzing case studies like this one not only highlights the measurable impacts of effective policy evaluations but also serves as an inspiration for readers to apply similar techniques in their projects. For instance, a small town grappling with high rates of youth unemployment might look to successful job training programs implemented elsewhere. By studying these initiatives, they can uncover best practices and identify potential pitfalls, ultimately tailoring a solution that fits their unique context. These real-world examples build a compelling narrative for advocacy, illustrating how targeted policy interventions can lead to significant positive changes.

Documenting successes helps illustrate the potential benefits of thorough policy evaluations and encourages local engagement. When community members see the concrete results of well-executed policies, they are more likely to participate in future projects and support ongoing initiatives. For example, a neighborhood revitalization project that documented its successes through before-and-after photos, testimonials from residents, and statistical improvements in crime reduction and property values, can effectively galvanize the community. People are motivated by visible, positive changes in their environment, and documented success stories serve as powerful tools for rallying support and fostering a sense of collective achievement.

Examining specific evaluative methods provides practical techniques for readers, showing actionable steps for their assessments. For instance, logic models can be instrumental in mapping out the relationships between resources, activities, and expected outcomes in policy implementation. By visualizing these connections, policymakers can better understand how specific inputs result in desired outcomes, making the evaluation process more straightforward. Moreover, logic models facilitate communication among stakeholders about the policy process, ensuring everyone is aligned and informed.

Another effective evaluative method is the use of cost-benefit analysis. This technique assesses economic impacts by weighing the total expected costs against anticipated benefits, driving the prioritization of initiatives that maximize social good. For instance, a city considering the implementation of a new public park could use a cost-benefit analysis to determine if the long-term health, environmental, and social benefits outweigh the initial costs. By transparently showcasing these calculations, policymakers can build trust within the community and justify their decisions with clear, data-driven evidence.

In addition to quantitative methods, qualitative research can provide deeper insights into community experiences with policies. Techniques such as interviews and focus groups reveal the nuanced perspectives of those directly affected by the policies, adding empathy and depth to the evaluation findings. For example, a social program aimed at supporting single parents may collect quantitative data on employment rates and income levels. Still, without qualitative input from the participants about their daily struggles and successes, the evaluation would lack a holistic understanding of the program's impact. Combining both types of data offers a richer, more comprehensive view of policy effectiveness.

A critical component of successful evaluations is the ability to communicate findings effectively. Data visualization tools like charts, graphs, and infographics can transform complex information into easily understandable formats, making it accessible to diverse audiences. For instance, an infographic summarizing the key outcomes of a health intervention program—such as increased vaccination rates or reduced hospital admissions—can quickly convey the program's success to policymakers, stakeholders, and the general public. Effective communication fosters transparency and builds confidence in the evaluation process.

To further enhance the evaluation efforts, familiarity with publicly available data sources is essential. Local, state, and federal databases offer a wealth of information that can be leveraged for policy assessments. For example, a community looking to address food insecurity might utilize demographic data, economic indicators, and health statistics from government databases to identify areas of greatest need and measure the impact of their interventions over time. Access to reliable data enables communities to make informed decisions and track progress accurately.

Case Studies of Successful Policy Evaluations – State Level

Examining effective state-level policy evaluations is crucial in drawing lessons for systemic change that can be applied to local initiatives. By understanding success stories from various state reforms, especially in health or education systems, we gain insight into how comprehensive evaluations at a larger scale can drive meaningful changes. For example, when analyzing the improvement of a state's healthcare system through expanded Medicaid services and preventive care programs, we observe a direct correlation between systematic evaluation efforts and improved health outcomes for residents.

These state-level success stories provide a wealth of knowledge that community members can adapt to their local initiatives. State reforms often have access to extensive resources and broader-reaching impacts, but the methodologies employed can still be scaled down effectively. For instance, if a state successfully employs data collection techniques to track student performance improvements in its education system, similar methods can be used by local school districts to monitor and enhance their educational practices. This adaptation fosters a sense of possibility in local activism, encouraging community members to believe that meaningful change is achievable within their own local context.

Adapting these techniques not only empowers community efforts but also provides concrete examples for implementing similar practices locally. Community leaders can look at specific instances where state-level policy evaluations have led to significant improvements and use those as blueprints. For example, a state's successful campaign to reduce smoking rates through public health education and taxation policies can serve as a model for a local initiative aiming to address teen vaping. Evaluating these success stories offers tangible strategies that are grounded in proven results, making them highly valuable for local activists and organizers.

Discussing the specific tools and methodologies employed in these state-level evaluations reveals the diversity of approaches available for robust assessments. One prominent tool is cost-benefit analysis, which assesses the economic impacts of policies by weighing total expected costs against anticipated benefits. This technique drives the prioritization of policy initiatives that maximize social good. It provides a clear financial perspective for policymakers and community members alike, allowing for more informed decision-making.

For example, in evaluating a state's transportation infrastructure upgrades, a cost-benefit analysis might consider the long-term savings from reduced vehicle maintenance and accident rates, alongside immediate construction costs. Understanding this balanced approach helps local stakeholders make better decisions regarding investments in their own community projects.

Another key methodology is the use of surveys and focus groups to gather qualitative data. This approach was successfully utilized in a state-level education reform initiative where stakeholders including teachers, parents, and students were actively engaged in providing feedback on curriculum changes. By collecting firsthand accounts and subjective experiences, evaluators gained deep insights into the community's needs and preferences, ultimately leading to more effective policy adjustments. Local initiatives can similarly benefit from employing qualitative research methods to garner rich, nuanced perspectives that guide their efforts.

Data visualization tools like charts and infographics are also prominent in state-level evaluations. These tools transform complex data sets into easily understandable visual formats, enhancing communication and advocacy. For instance, a state's public health department might use an infographic to illustrate the impact of vaccination programs on disease reduction. When local communities adopt such visualization techniques, they make their findings accessible to a wider audience, thereby increasing public engagement and support for their policies.

In addition to these methodologies, another critical aspect of state-level evaluations is the emphasis on longitudinal studies. By examining data over extended periods, states can track the sustained effects of policies, identifying trends and long-term outcomes. A state that implements a new standardized testing method in schools might conduct a ten-year study to observe changes in academic performance and college admission rates. Local initiatives can learn from this approach by committing to ongoing assessments of their policies, ensuring that they remain effective and relevant over time.

Furthermore, transparency and inclusivity are cornerstones of effective policy evaluations at the state level. Successful states often prioritize open communication with the public and involve diverse stakeholder groups throughout the evaluation process. In a state environmental policy assessment, for example, involving community organizations, industry representatives, and environmental scientists can lead to more balanced and accepted outcomes. Local initiatives should emulate this model by fostering transparent practices and encouraging broad community participation in their evaluations.

Ultimately, examining effective state-level policy evaluations offers invaluable lessons for driving systemic change within local initiatives. By understanding state success stories and adapting their techniques, community members can harness proven methodologies to address local challenges. Insights gleaned from these evaluations serve as practical examples, guiding local activists and organizers towards impactful solutions. Moreover, discussing the array of tools and methodologies used at the state level reveals a toolkit of diverse approaches, equipping local stakeholders with the knowledge needed for robust and effective policy evaluations.

Case Studies of Successful Policy Evaluations – National Level

Evaluating national policy's impacts is crucial to understanding how broad legislative measures influence different segments of society. This section aims to delve into the importance of ongoing evaluation throughout policy implementation, providing insights into broader legislative trends.

National case studies are invaluable for contextualizing local efforts within the larger political landscape. For example, examining the success or failure of specific national policies can highlight the strengths and weaknesses inherent in those policies. By studying these cases, community leaders and activists can learn from past mistakes and replicate successful strategies on a local scale. Case studies also illustrate how policies interact with diverse social, economic, and political conditions, offering a nuanced view of their effectiveness.

When it comes to evaluating the impacts of national policies on vulnerable populations, it's essential to adopt both quantitative and qualitative research methods. Quantitative data collection involves gathering numerical data through surveys, demographic studies, and economic indicators. This data provides an objective basis for evaluating policy impacts. For instance, a national health policy might show improved health outcomes through reduced mortality rates and increased access to healthcare services. Conversely, qualitative research methods like interviews and focus groups reveal deep insights into how these policies affect individuals and communities on a personal level. By combining these approaches, we gain a comprehensive understanding of the real-world implications of national policies.

The ability to share lessons learned from national contexts equips readers with valuable knowledge for conducting local assessments. National evaluations often come with well-documented processes and results, which serve as educational resources for local policymakers and activists. These documented lessons help identify what works and what doesn't, enabling more effective policy design and implementation at the local level. For instance, if a national housing policy successfully reduces homelessness, analyzing its key components can guide local authorities in developing similar initiatives tailored to their unique circumstances.

One practical tool for enhancing policy evaluation is using templates or outlines derived from national scenarios. These standardized tools assist in implementing methodologically sound evaluations across various civic engagements. Templates provide a structured approach to data collection, analysis, and reporting, ensuring consistency and rigor in evaluations. For example, a template designed for assessing education policies might include sections for identifying key performance indicators, collecting relevant data, and interpreting the findings. Such tools simplify the evaluation process, making it accessible even to those with limited experience in policy analysis.

Quantitative data collection, as mentioned earlier, plays a pivotal role in informing policy analysis. Gathering numerical data allows evaluators to measure policy impacts accurately and objectively.

This data can be visualized through charts and infographics, effectively communicating insights to diverse audiences. Whether presenting findings to community members or stakeholders, clear and visually appealing data representations enhance understanding and engagement. For instance, a bar chart comparing dropout rates before and after implementing an education policy can vividly illustrate the policy's impact on student retention.

Qualitative research methods are equally important in revealing the human side of policy impacts. Techniques such as interviews and focus groups bring out the experiences, feelings, and perceptions of those affected by the policies. These narratives add depth to quantitative findings, fostering empathy and a more nuanced understanding of the issues at hand. For example, while numerical data might show a reduction in poverty levels following a welfare policy, interviews with beneficiaries can uncover challenges they still face and areas needing improvement. These personal stories resonate with policymakers, driving more informed and compassionate decision-making.

Data visualization tools are not just useful but necessary for communicating complex data insights. Charts, graphs, and infographics translate dense numerical information into easily digestible visuals. These tools make it easier for audiences to grasp trends, patterns, and key messages quickly. Imagine a policymaker presenting data on climate change impacts; a series of heat maps showing temperature changes over decades can powerfully convey the urgency of the issue compared to a table full of numbers. Effective data visualization bridges the gap between detailed analysis and public comprehension, enhancing advocacy efforts.

Access to publicly available data sources is another critical aspect of robust policy evaluation. Knowledge of local, state, and federal databases enables evaluators to gather comprehensive information required for thorough assessments. Databases such as census records, public health reports, and economic surveys offer rich data sets that inform evaluations. For instance, accessing crime statistics from federal databases can help evaluate the effectiveness of a national criminal justice reform policy. Familiarity with these resources fosters transparency and accountability in governance, empowering citizens and community leaders alike to engage in informed civic activities.

Final Thoughts

In this chapter, we have explored various interactive methods for evaluating local policies and their impacts. By delving into tools such as Stakeholder Analysis, SWOT Analysis, Logic Models, and Cost-Benefit Analysis, readers are now equipped with practical frameworks for assessing community policies effectively. These methods enable a thorough examination of the diverse interests, potential strengths and weaknesses, and the economic feasibility of proposed initiatives. Moreover, we've discussed how these tools offer a structured approach to understanding policy outcomes, helping to ensure that policies are not only inclusive but also efficient and beneficial to all stakeholders.

Understanding these evaluation techniques empowers individuals to make informed decisions and advocate for necessary changes within their communities. Equipped with both quantitative and qualitative research methods, community members can gather comprehensive data and personal experiences to build a robust analysis of local policies. Additionally, effective data visualization enhances the communication of complex information, making it accessible to a broader audience. Leveraging publicly available data sources further strengthens evaluations, fostering transparency and accountability in governance. Through these efforts, readers are better prepared to engage in civic activities, driving positive changes and creating more equitable communities.

<h1 style="text-align:center">CHAPTER 6</h1>

Organizing Impactful Eventsand Campaigns

Organizing impactful events and campaigns is vital for driving community engagement and achieving civic goals. The ability to meticulously plan and execute these events can significantly influence their success and the extent of their impact within the community. Events that are thoroughly planned resonate more with participants and ensure that all logistical details are managed effectively, creating a memorable experience that fosters long-term involvement and support.

In this chapter, readers will receive detailed guidance on every aspect of organizing successful civic events and campaigns. It begins by emphasizing the importance of defining clear objectives and outcomes, which provides a focused direction for the planning process. The chapter also covers essential logistics such as budgeting, venue selection, and scheduling, ensuring that no detail is overlooked. Moreover, it addresses the technical requirements and permits needed, as well as safety measures to ensure smooth execution. Additionally, the chapter highlights the importance of engaging community members throughout the process and suggests strategies for post-event reflection and appreciation. By the end of this chapter, readers will be equipped with practical skills and knowledge to create events that leave a lasting positive impact on their communities.

Event Planning and Logistics

Planning and executing impactful events is a critical skill for anyone involved in civic activities or community engagement. Effective event planning not only ensures that all logistical aspects are covered, but also that the event resonates with the target audience, creating lasting community impact. Here's a step-by-step guide to mastering the essential elements of effective event planning.

Identify the Purpose and Desired Outcomes

To start, it's essential to clearly identify the purpose and desired outcomes of your event. Ask yourself, what do you hope to achieve? Whether it's raising awareness on an issue, fundraising, educating the public, or mobilizing community action, understanding your goals helps keep your planning process focused. For instance, if your advocacy aims to increase voter registration, your event could focus on providing information booths, registration stations, and speakers who can inspire action. Having clear objectives will guide every decision you make, from the type of activities you include to the promotional strategies you employ.

Create a Comprehensive Budget

Next, create a detailed budget accounting for all potential expenses and sources of income. This includes venue rental, permits, promotional materials, refreshments, equipment rentals, travel expenses for speakers, and staff or volunteer compensation. It's also crucial to identify revenue streams such as entry fees, donations, and sponsorships. Make sure to research and reach out to potential sponsors well in advance, presenting them with compelling reasons to support your event. For example, local businesses might be willing to sponsor if they see the alignment between their brand values and your cause. A thorough budget helps prevent unexpected costs and ensures you have the necessary funds to execute your event successfully.

Choose the Right Venue

Selecting an appropriate location is another key factor. The venue should be accessible and suitable for the activities planned. Consider the size, facilities, parking availability, and public transportation options. If you're hosting a health fair, for example, you might choose a community center with multiple rooms for different types of screenings, talks, and fitness demos. Configuring the venue to create an engaging environment is equally important; think about the layout, decorations, signage, and seating arrangements that will best support the flow and feel of your event. The right setup can significantly enhance attendee experience, making your event more memorable and impactful.

Plan the Event Flow

Effective logistics management involves planning the flow of the event meticulously. Outline a detailed schedule outlining each segment of the event, from setup to teardown. This schedule should include specific times for activities like guest arrivals, opening remarks, key presentations, breakout sessions, and breaks. Ensure that you allocate sufficient time for transitions between different parts of the event to avoid feeling rushed. For a rally or protest, this might include arranging for sound systems, stages, and ensuring the route is safe and well-coordinated.

In addition, consider all technical requirements. This ranges from audio-visual needs like microphones, projectors, and speakers, to internet connectivity for live streaming or social media updates. Ensure someone on your team is responsible for overseeing these technical aspects to handle any issues that may arise swiftly.

Obtaining necessary permits and adhering to safety measures is non-negotiable. Depending on the type and scale of your event, you'll need to secure various permits, which might include those for sound amplification, road closures, or selling food and beverages. Check with local authorities to understand the requirements well ahead of time. Additionally, prioritize safety by having a plan for crowd control, first aid, emergency exits, and addressing potential security concerns. Hiring professional security personnel for large events or liaising with local law enforcement can help ensure everything runs smoothly.

Engage Your Community

Throughout the planning process, continuously seek ways to engage your community. Involve them early by inviting input on what kind of events they would like to see and incorporating their ideas wherever feasible. Engagement fosters a sense of ownership and investment in the event's success. Utilize various communication channels to keep the community informed and excited about upcoming events. Regular updates through social media, newsletters, and local newspapers can build anticipation and ensure a good turnout.

Consider forming committees or working groups that represent different segments of your community. These groups can provide diverse perspectives and help distribute the workload, making the planning process more manageable and inclusive.

Post-Event Activities

After the event, take time to reflect on what went well and areas for improvement. Gathering feedback from attendees, volunteers, and partners is invaluable. Distribute surveys, hold debrief meetings, and review metrics such as attendance numbers, funds raised, and social media engagement. This information will be crucial for planning future events and demonstrating your success to stakeholders and potential sponsors.

Ensure you acknowledge and thank everyone who contributed to the event's success. Publicly recognizing volunteers, donors, and partners not only shows appreciation but also strengthens relationships and encourages continued support for future initiatives.

Strategies for Effective Marketing and Promotion

Understanding your audience is a fundamental aspect of effectively promoting civic events and campaigns. Knowing who your event is for enables you to tailor your promotional efforts to engage the right demographics. Start by identifying your target audience; this could be students, local community members, or a broader public interested in the issues your event addresses. Conduct surveys or use existing data to gather information about their interests, behaviors, and preferred communication channels. For example, if your event aims to raise awareness about climate change, target groups that are already concerned with environmental issues.

Once you have identified your audience, craft messages that resonate with them. Use language and visuals that appeal to their values and interests. Highlight aspects of the event that would most likely attract their attention, such as keynote speakers, interactive workshops, or networking opportunities. Personalizing your outreach can significantly increase engagement and attendance.

Leveraging social media platforms is another critical strategy for promoting your event. Social media allows you to reach a wider audience and create buzz around your event. Start by choosing the right platforms based on where your target audience spends their time. Popular choices include Facebook, Twitter, Instagram, and LinkedIn. Each platform has its strengths—Facebook is great for creating events and engaging with detailed posts, while Instagram is useful for sharing visually appealing content like photos and videos.

Create a content calendar to plan your social media posts leading up to the event. Include a mix of content types such as announcements, behind-the-scenes preparations, speaker highlights, and attendee testimonials. Engage with your audience by responding to comments and encouraging them to share your posts. Utilize hashtags related to your event to increase visibility and join relevant online conversations. Additionally, consider using paid ads to boost your outreach and target specific demographics more precisely.

Designing eye-catching visuals and authentic content is essential for capturing and maintaining the interest of your potential attendees. Visuals are often the first thing people notice, so make sure they are compelling and aligned with your event's theme. Use high-quality images, graphics, and videos to convey the event's purpose and tone. Tools like Canva or Adobe Spark can help you create professional-looking visuals even if you don't have a design background.

Authentic content goes beyond just attractive visuals—it involves telling a genuine story about why your event matters. Share personal anecdotes or case studies that highlight the impact of your cause. For instance, if your event focuses on mental health awareness, share stories from individuals who have benefited from similar initiatives. Authenticity helps build trust and emotional connections with your audience, making them more likely to attend and support your event.

Collaborating with local organizations, influencers, and media can significantly broaden your outreach and lend credibility to your event. Partner with organizations that align with your event's goals and can help promote it through their networks. For example, if you're organizing a community clean-up, collaborate with environmental groups, local businesses, and schools. These partners can assist with spreading the word and may provide additional resources such as volunteers or funding.

Influencers can amplify your message to a larger audience. Identify key influencers within your community or industry who share your event's values. Reach out to them with a clear proposal outlining how they can contribute, whether it's through social media shout-outs, blog posts, or attending the event themselves. In return, offer them recognition or other incentives such as free tickets or exclusive access.

Engaging with local media is also vital. Send press releases to newspapers, radio stations, and TV channels well in advance. Highlight the uniqueness of your event and its relevance to the community. Offer interviews with key organizers or speakers to provide deeper insights. Media coverage can attract more attendees and add a layer of legitimacy to your event.

Identifying Potential Sponsors

Acquiring financial support and sponsorship for events and campaigns is a crucial step in ensuring their success and sustainability. Here are some practical strategies that will help you secure the necessary funds and build long-term partnerships.

First, conduct thorough research to identify businesses or organizations whose goals and values align with your event or campaign. This alignment is essential because it increases the likelihood of gaining their support. Start by exploring local companies known for community involvement or those with Corporate Social Responsibility (CSR) programs. Engage with online networks such as LinkedIn to find potential sponsors who share your mission. Doing this groundwork helps create a targeted list of prospects, making the entire sponsorship process more efficient and effective.

Once you have identified potential sponsors, the next step is to develop compelling proposals. A well-crafted proposal should clearly outline the benefits and engagement opportunities for the sponsor. Highlight how supporting your event will enhance their brand visibility, offer marketing opportunities, and create positive social impact. Include data, testimonials, or past successes to add credibility. Visual aids like infographics can make your proposal more engaging. Remember, a detailed and clear proposal demonstrates professionalism and increases the chances of securing sponsorships.

Beyond traditional sponsorships, exploring community-based fundraising strategies can significantly boost your event funding. Grassroots efforts can mobilize a wider section of the community, creating a sense of shared ownership and support. Organize events like car washes, bake sales, or talent shows where community members can actively participate and contribute. Utilize online crowdfunding platforms such as GoFundMe or Kickstarter to reach a broader audience. These platforms allow you to tell your story, set fundraising goals, and engage with supporters through updates and rewards. Community-based fundraising not only raises money but also builds a loyal base of supporters who feel invested in your cause.

Maintaining communication with sponsors and funders post-event is critical for nurturing these relationships and securing future opportunities. Begin by sending personalized thank-you notes to express gratitude for their support. Provide them with detailed reports on how their contributions were utilized and the impact achieved. Share photos, videos, and testimonials from the event to bring the experience to life. Regularly update them on future projects and invite them to participate in planning stages to keep them engaged. Building strong, ongoing relationships with sponsors ensures a reliable foundation for future events and campaigns.

It's important to highlight that while financial support is vital, so is the transparency and accountability of how funds are used. Keep meticulous records of all expenses and donations. Being transparent about financial matters will build trust and encourage continued support.

Leveraging Grassroots Fundraising

Enhancing financial resilience through community initiatives is crucial for the long-term success of impactful events and campaigns. By actively involving community members in funding activities, you can create a sense of ownership and commitment that not only boosts financial resources but also strengthens communal bonds. One effective way to build this sense of ownership is by engaging community members in various fundraising activities.

When individuals participate in these activities, they feel personally invested in the cause, making them more likely to contribute both time and resources. For example, organizing neighborhood meetings to discuss funding needs and brainstorm ideas can serve as a great starting point. Participants could be encouraged to contribute their skills, whether it's baking goods for a sale or offering services for an auction. These collaborative efforts help in creating a shared vision and a stronger connection to the community's goals.

Diversifying fundraising strategies is another essential tactic to ensure overall financial stability. Relying on a single source of income is risky; hence, having multiple streams can safeguard against potential shortfalls. Consider combining traditional methods like car washes and bake sales with modern approaches such as online crowdfunding. Each strategy has its unique advantages and can cater to different segments of the community.

Organizing community-based events is a practical approach to diversify your fundraising efforts. Events like car washes, bake sales, or donation drives not only generate funds but also provide opportunities for community engagement and visibility. A car wash, for instance, can bring together students, local businesses, and residents, providing them with an opportunity to collaborate and bond over a shared goal. Similarly, bake sales allow participants to showcase their culinary talents while raising money for the cause. Donation drives are particularly effective for collecting goods and services that can be sold or used directly by those in need.

Each event requires careful planning and execution to maximize its impact. For example, setting up a dedicated team to handle logistics, promotions, and volunteer coordination can greatly enhance the efficiency of the event. Advertising via social media, local newspapers, and community bulletin boards ensures that the turnout is significant, thereby increasing the amount raised.

Utilizing online crowdfunding platforms is another powerful tool to tap into a wider audience. Platforms like GoFundMe, Kickstarter, and Indiegogo allow you to reach people beyond your immediate geographic area. Creating a compelling story about your cause, complete with visuals and testimonials, can attract donations from individuals who share your passion but may not reside locally. Crowdfunding also enables you to set specific targets and milestones, providing donors with clear goals to work towards.

The key to successful crowdfunding lies in consistent updates and communication. Regularly informing your backers about the progress of your campaign fosters trust and encourages continued support. Sharing stories of how the funds are making a difference can inspire others to contribute as well, creating a ripple effect that extends your reach even further.

Another advantage of online crowdfunding is the ability to utilize social media to amplify your message. Encouraging your supporters to share your campaign on their social networks can exponentially increase its visibility. Social media challenges, live-streaming events, and interactive posts can engage your audience, keeping the momentum going throughout the fundraising period.

Follow-Up and Relationship Management

Post-event actions play a crucial role in building long-term partnerships. These actions not only solidify the efforts invested in the event but also pave the way for future collaborations and stronger community ties. One of the most effective ways to foster these relationships is by demonstrating appreciation. Sending thank-you notes, crafting detailed reports, and making public acknowledgments can go a long way in showing gratitude. When sponsors, partners, and volunteers see that their contributions are valued, they feel more connected to your cause and are likely to support future initiatives.

Thank-you notes, whether handwritten or digital, provide a personal touch that reinforces the impact each individual or organization had on the event's success. Acknowledging sponsors and partners publicly, such as during the event's closing remarks or through social media posts, also showcases your appreciation to a broader audience. Additionally, post-event reports detailing the event's outcomes, participation metrics, and any media coverage serve as tangible evidence of success, reinforcing the importance of each partner's contribution.

To maintain these valuable partnerships, regular check-ins and updates are essential. Scheduling periodic meetings or sending out newsletters helps keep sponsors engaged and informed about ongoing projects and future plans. These interactions should be more than just updates; they should include conversations about how both parties can continue to benefit from the partnership. By staying in constant communication, you ensure that sponsors feel involved and appreciated, which in turn encourages their continued support.

Soliciting feedback from partners and attendees is another critical step in post-event actions. Feedback provides insight into what worked well and what areas need improvement. This information is invaluable for planning future events and campaigns. Creating surveys or hosting debrief meetings can facilitate this process. Ensure that you have a system in place to collect, analyze, and act on this feedback. Showing that you take their opinions seriously and make changes based on their input will strengthen trust and collaboration.

Showcasing successful outcomes and impacts effectively validates the support received while inspiring confidence in future endeavors. Sharing success stories through various channels such as social media, newsletters, or community meetings highlights the tangible benefits of their involvement. Use data and personal anecdotes to illustrate the positive changes brought about by the event. Whether it's an increase in community engagement, policy changes, or improved local services, make sure to communicate these successes clearly.

Consider creating case studies or impact reports that detail how specific contributions led to particular successes. These documents can be shared with current and potential partners to demonstrate the value and effectiveness of your efforts. Highlighting these achievements not only affirms past support but also serves as a persuasive tool for garnering future backing.

In addition to these methods, it's important to foster a sense of community among your partners and supporters. Organize networking events, appreciation dinners, or informal gatherings where partners can connect, share ideas, and explore new collaboration opportunities. Building a community around your cause ensures that partnerships are not just transactional but deeply rooted in mutual respect and shared goals.

Long-term partnerships thrive on mutual benefits and shared success. By routinely showcasing appreciation, maintaining open lines of communication, seeking constructive feedback, and celebrating successes together, you cultivate strong, enduring relationships. These relationships form the backbone of impactful civic events and campaigns, ensuring sustained community engagement and support.

Lastly, alignment in vision and goals between your organization and its partners is vital. Regularly revisit and reaffirm the shared objectives that brought you together in the first place. Ensuring that everyone remains committed to the same mission keeps the partnership aligned and focused on achieving greater impact.

Summary and Reflections

This chapter has offered a comprehensive guide on how to plan and execute civic events that make a significant impact in the community. By focusing on key elements such as identifying the event's purpose, creating a budget, choosing the right venue, and managing logistics, you are equipped to handle the complexities of event planning efficiently. Additionally, engaging your community in the process ensures better participation and support, while post-event activities like gathering feedback and acknowledging contributors help build strong relationships for future events.

Implementing these strategies can greatly enhance the effectiveness and reach of your civic initiatives. Whether you're raising awareness, mobilizing action, or simply bringing people together, attention to detail in every planning stage is crucial. Remember, the success of an event isn't just in its execution but also in how well it resonates with your community and achieves the desired outcomes. With thorough planning, clear objectives, and active community involvement, your events will not only be impactful but also pave the way for sustained civic engagement and support.

CHAPTER 7

Tools for Effective Advocacy

Effective advocacy requires a solid grasp of the tools and strategies needed to create change. This chapter will guide readers through the essential elements necessary for impactful advocacy, including crafting effective plans, developing strong communication skills, and building robust coalitions. Understanding the dynamics at play in different advocacy environments helps ensure that efforts are tailored to make the greatest impact.

To equip readers with practical insights, the chapter delves into creating well-structured advocacy plans and agendas. Readers will learn how to navigate various levels of advocacy, from local to national, by understanding stakeholder mapping and setting SMART goals. The chapter also covers the importance of community needs in goal setting and how to develop detailed action plans. Additionally, it explores public speaking techniques, methods for handling objections, and the significance of practice and feedback in honing advocacy skills. Finally, it emphasizes the value of coalition-building, providing strategies for identifying partners, establishing roles, and leveraging collective resources for more significant outcomes.

Creating Advocacy Plans and Agendas

Understanding the advocacy landscape requires a deep dive into the different environments where advocacy plays out. Awareness of these settings is essential for crafting effective strategies and forming realistic goals. Advocacy can occur at local, state, and national levels, each with its unique characteristics and challenges.

Local advocacy may involve engaging with city councils or community boards to influence decisions that directly impact neighborhoods. State-level advocacy often requires navigating more complex legislative processes and forming coalitions with other organizations to amplify efforts. National advocacy involves interacting with federal agencies and policymakers, requiring an understanding of broader political contexts and national issues.

For example, a campaign aiming to address homelessness might have distinct approaches at each level. At the local level, advocates could push for better funding for shelters. At the state level, they might work on policies addressing affordable housing. At the national level, they might engage in lobbying for legislation improving nationwide housing assistance programs. Understanding these layers ensures advocates can effectively tailor their efforts to the right audience and leverage appropriate resources.

Stakeholder mapping is another critical exercise in understanding the advocacy landscape. This process helps identify key allies and opponents, offering a clear picture of who can support your cause and who might resist it. Allies might include community leaders, nonprofit organizations, and sympathetic policymakers, while opponents could range from industry groups to certain political factions. Identifying stakeholders allows advocates to develop tailored strategies for engagement and opposition management. For instance, if pushing for environmental regulations, an advocate needs to know which businesses might oppose the regulations and which environmental groups can provide support and resources.

Setting SMART goals is the next vital step. SMART stands for Specific, Measurable, Achievable, Relevant, and Time-bound. These criteria help formulate clear and actionable objectives. A specific goal addresses a precise aspect of an issue rather than a broad, vague intention. For example, instead of aiming to "improve education," a SMART goal would be "to increase the graduation rate of underprivileged students in X district by 10% within two years."

Measureability ensures the goal's progress can be tracked, providing milestones to gauge success. The achievability criterion reminds advocates to set realistic expectations, preventing burnout and maintaining motivation. Relevance ties the goal to broader movements or trends, ensuring the effort contributes meaningfully to larger causes. Finally, time-bound goals include deadlines, creating urgency and a framework for planning and execution.

Community needs play a crucial role in setting SMART goals. By aligning goals with what the community genuinely requires, advocates ensure their efforts are meaningful and impactful. For instance, if a community suffers from high unemployment rates, a relevant advocacy goal might focus on job creation initiatives or vocational training programs. Additionally, aligning goals with broader trends or movements amplifies the impact, as it connects local efforts to national or global campaigns, creating a ripple effect of change.

Developing action plans transforms goals into tangible steps. An action plan should outline tasks, assign responsibilities, and establish timelines. This detailed roadmap guides the team, ensuring everyone knows their roles and deadlines. For instance, if the goal is to organize a public awareness campaign about climate change, the action plan might include tasks such as designing promotional materials, securing venues for events, reaching out to speakers, and scheduling social media posts.

Considering logistical aspects and resource allocation is also crucial. This involves determining what resources—time, money, and manpower—are needed and how they will be used. For instance, if organizing a large-scale event, planning must account for venue costs, transportation, promotional materials, and volunteer coordination. Efficient resource allocation prevents wastage and ensures all necessary elements are in place for smooth execution.

Using planning tools and templates can streamline this process. Tools like Gantt charts, spreadsheets, and project management software help visualize the timeline and track progress. Templates provide standardized formats for creating comprehensive plans, ensuring consistency and clarity. These tools not only aid in organizing tasks but also facilitate communication among team members, keeping everyone aligned and informed.

Evaluating effectiveness is the final step, focusing on assessing the success of advocacy efforts. Evaluation criteria or metrics might include quantitative measures such as attendance numbers, participation rates, or policy changes achieved. Qualitative feedback, like testimonials or surveys, provides insights into the perceived impact and areas for improvement. Collecting and analyzing these outcomes offers a holistic view of what worked well and what didn't.

For example, if the goal was to educate the community about health risks, metrics could include the number of educational sessions held, attendance figures, and pre-and post-event surveys assessing knowledge gain. Feedback from participants might reveal whether the information was accessible and engaging or if adjustments are needed.

Iterating strategies based on feedback ensures continuous improvement. Advocacy is an evolving field, and flexibility is key to adapting to changing circumstances and new information. Regularly revisiting goals, plans, and evaluation methods keeps efforts relevant and effective. For instance, if a particular strategy didn't yield the desired results, analyzing why it failed and making necessary adjustments can enhance future initiatives.

Utilizing Public Speaking and Persuasion Techniques

Equipping yourself with the skills needed for impactful public speaking is essential for effective advocacy. Effective communication can significantly enhance your ability to persuade various audiences, whether you are addressing a small group or speaking to a larger crowd. This subpoint will provide you with valuable insights on crafting compelling messages, using engagement techniques, handling objections and questions, and the importance of practice and feedback.

Crafting Compelling Messages

One of the first steps in public speaking for advocacy is crafting messages that resonate deeply with your audience. The key here is to balance emotion, logic, and storytelling elements. You need to make sure your message stirs emotions, appeals to reason, and tells a story that people can relate to.

Start by identifying the core message you want to convey. What is the main point you want your audience to remember? From there, build your narrative. Use personal anecdotes or real-life examples to humanize your message, making it more relatable and memorable. Emotional stories tend to linger in people's minds far longer than impersonal data points.

While emotion plays a crucial role, logical arguments are equally important. Data, statistics, and factual evidence lend credibility to your message. However, be concise and clear; avoid overwhelming your audience with too many details. Balance is key—too much emotion without logic can seem insubstantial, while too much logic without emotion can be dry and unengaging.

Engagement Techniques

Once you have crafted your message, the next challenge is delivering it in a way that keeps your audience engaged. Interactive strategies can make a significant difference here. Asking questions during your presentation invites participation and keeps the audience mentally involved. For instance, posing rhetorical questions can stimulate thought and emphasize key points.

Body language and voice modulation are other critical aspects of engaging your audience. Maintain eye contact to create a connection with your listeners. Use gestures to emphasize important points but avoid overdoing them, as this can be distracting. Your voice should have variety—vary your pitch, speed, and volume to maintain interest and underscore different parts of your speech.

Visual aids can be extremely effective in keeping your audience engaged and helping them understand complex topics. Slides, charts, and videos can break the monotony and add a visual dimension to your message. However, ensure that your visuals are clear, relevant, and not overly cluttered.

Handling Objections and Questions

Public speaking often involves addressing objections and questions from the audience. This is especially true in advocacy, where differing viewpoints are common. Being well-prepared to handle these challenges is crucial.

When faced with objections, listen actively and respond respectfully. Acknowledge the concerns raised, even if you don't agree with them. This shows that you value the opinions of your audience, which can make them more receptive to your viewpoint. Formulate your responses carefully, using facts and logic to counter objections while also appealing to underlying emotions.

During debates or Q&A sessions, it's essential to remain calm and composed. Hostile questions or objections can rattle even seasoned speakers. Take a moment to think before responding. If you don't know the answer to a question, it's better to admit it rather than provide incorrect information. You can always offer to follow up later with a detailed response.

Practice and Feedback

No matter how well-crafted your message or how effective your engagement techniques, nothing can replace the value of practice and feedback. Rehearsing your speech multiple times helps you become familiar with the content and reduces the likelihood of stumbling over words. Practice in front of a mirror to observe your body language and facial expressions.

Seek constructive critique from peers, mentors, or coaches. They can offer valuable insights into areas where you can improve. Constructive feedback can highlight aspects you might not have considered, such as pacing, tone, or clarity.

Building confidence through practice is a gradual process, but it's immensely rewarding. The more you practice, the more comfortable you become with your material and your delivery. Reflection after each speaking opportunity is also vital. Assess what went well and what could be improved for next time.

Building Coalitions for Greater Impact

Collaboration and coalition-building are crucial in advocacy work because they unite individuals and organizations towards shared goals, creating a stronger and more influential force for social change. A united front amplifies the impact of advocacy efforts, making it easier to achieve common objectives and drive meaningful progress.

Identifying potential coalition partners is a foundational step in building a powerful advocacy coalition. It begins by selecting organizations and individuals whose values and missions align with the overarching advocacy goals. This alignment ensures that all parties are working towards a common cause and that their efforts will be mutually reinforcing. Incorporating diversity within the coalition is equally important, as it brings a range of perspectives and experiences to the table. Diversity enhances creativity, broadens the appeal of the advocacy message, and better represents the varied stakeholders involved or affected by the issue at hand.

Once potential partners are identified, establishing clear roles and responsibilities is essential for maintaining an organized and efficient coalition. Outlining expectations and contributions for each member helps prevent overlaps and gaps in tasks, ensuring that every aspect of the advocacy campaign is covered. Creating a coalition charter can formalize these roles and responsibilities, serving as a reference document that outlines the coalition's mission, objectives, and operational guidelines. Effective communication and transparency are critical components in this process. Regular updates, meetings, and open channels of communication help maintain trust among members and keep everyone informed and engaged.

Leveraging collective resources is a significant advantage of coalition-building. By pooling resources, knowledge, and networks, coalition members can achieve greater impact than if they were working independently. Shared resources might include funding, expertise, technology, and access to broader networks. Joint fundraising efforts can significantly boost the financial capabilities of the coalition, allowing for more extensive and effective advocacy activities. Resource allocation should be strategic, ensuring that resources are used where they will have the most significant effect. This might involve investing in research, outreach campaigns, or lobbying efforts that benefit the entire coalition.

Sustaining coalitions over time is a challenge but crucial for long-term success in advocacy work. Maintaining motivation and engagement among coalition members requires regular check-ins, celebrating small wins, and ensuring that members feel valued and heard. Conflict resolution mechanisms should be in place to address any disagreements that arise, ensuring that issues are resolved promptly and do not derail the coalition's efforts. It's also important to continue reaching out and building relationships with community stakeholders. These stakeholders can offer valuable support, insights, and resources, and keeping them engaged helps sustain the coalition's momentum and relevance.

Implementing these strategies can help build strong, resilient coalitions capable of driving significant social change. Identifying suitable partners based on aligned values, establishing clear roles, leveraging collective resources, and sustaining the coalition over time are all interdependent elements that contribute to the overall success of advocacy efforts. Coalition-building is not just about combining forces; it's about creating a synergistic relationship where the whole is greater than the sum of its parts.

By selecting partners who share your advocacy goals and embrace diverse perspectives, you can create a more inclusive and robust coalition. Establishing a structured framework for roles and responsibilities enhances operational efficiency and accountability. Effective communication and transparency foster trust and cooperation among members, laying the foundation for a cohesive team.

Pooling resources and knowledge maximizes the coalition's capacity to effect change, while joint fundraising efforts provide the necessary financial backing for large-scale initiatives. Strategic resource allocation ensures that efforts are focused on areas with the highest potential for impact, optimizing the use of available assets.

Sustaining the coalition's momentum requires ongoing effort to maintain motivation and resolve conflicts constructively. Regular engagement with community stakeholders enriches the coalition's perspectives and strengthens its support base, contributing to its resilience and adaptability.

Navigating Political Contexts

Understanding the political landscape surrounding advocacy issues is crucial for anyone looking to make a meaningful impact. By analyzing current policies, political climates, and key decision-makers, advocates can craft strategies that are both informed and effective.

Analyzing the political context begins with understanding the existing policies related to your issue. This includes examining legislation that has been enacted, proposed bills, and any ongoing regulatory processes. For example, if you are advocating for environmental protection, knowing the specifics of laws such as the Clean Air Act or Paris Agreement commitments will be vital. Researching these policies helps to identify gaps that need addressing, strengths that can be leveraged, and potential obstacles.

Equally important is an examination of the political climate. This refers to the overall mood, attitudes, and opinions prevalent among the populace and those in power. In periods of political stability, advocacy efforts may face fewer hurdles compared to times of upheaval or transition. For instance, during election years, policy priorities might shift, making it either easier or harder to push certain agendas. Understanding the political climate allows advocates to anticipate challenges and seize favorable opportunities for action.

Key decision-makers, such as elected officials, government leaders, and influential stakeholders, play a significant role in shaping outcomes. Identifying these individuals and their positions on relevant issues provides insight into how best to approach advocacy efforts. Advocates should aim to understand these leaders' motivations, values, and past voting records. Building profiles for each key decision-maker can guide strategy development, helping to tailor approaches that resonate with specific audiences.

Once the political context is clear, adapting messaging to different advocacy terrains becomes essential. Messaging must be tailored to suit local, state, or national political environments. At the local level, personal stories and community impact might hold more weight. For example, sharing how a new educational policy could affect local schools may gain traction with city council members. On a state or national level, broader themes such as economic benefits or public health improvements might prove more persuasive. Tailored messaging ensures that communications are relevant, compelling, and capable of engaging the intended audience effectively.

Influencing policymakers requires a deep understanding of legislative processes. Knowing how a bill becomes law, the committees involved, and the timelines for various stages means advocates can time their efforts strategically. Organizing targeted advocacy campaigns around critical junctures, such as committee hearings or floor votes, maximizes impact. Additionally, relationship-building with elected officials is fundamental. This involves regular communication, attending town hall meetings, and participating in constituent events. Personalized contact, such as sending letters or scheduling meetings, demonstrates commitment and helps build rapport.

Advocates should also focus on organizing targeted advocacy campaigns. These campaigns often include actions like letter-writing drives, public demonstrations, and social media initiatives. For instance, arranging a peaceful protest outside a senator's office can draw media attention and highlight the urgency of particular issues. Targeted campaigns ensure that efforts are concentrated where they can most influence decision-making, increasing the likelihood of achieving advocacy goals.

Monitoring political developments is another crucial aspect of effective advocacy. Staying informed about policy changes and political shifts allows advocates to adapt their strategies swiftly. This involves tracking legislative sessions, subscribing to news alerts, and following think tanks or advocacy groups that provide updates on relevant issues. For instance, if a sudden policy change impacts environmental regulations, immediate awareness enables advocates to respond quickly, whether by organizing a campaign or issuing a public statement.

Evaluating the effectiveness of advocacy efforts is equally important. This process involves setting benchmarks for success, collecting data, and analyzing outcomes. Feedback loops with constituents and stakeholders help gauge whether objectives are being met and identify areas for improvement. For example, after running a campaign to raise awareness about mental health services, gathering feedback through surveys can reveal which messages resonated most and what additional information might be needed. Regular evaluation ensures that advocacy remains responsive and impactful.

Understanding how to collect and analyze advocacy outcomes will also be discussed. This entails using tools like surveys, interviews, and data analysis software to gather quantitative and qualitative information. Advocacy outcomes might include changes in public opinion, policy shifts, or increased engagement from the target audience. Analyzing these outcomes helps determine the efficacy of different tactics and informs future strategies.

Readers will learn to pivot strategies based on evaluation results. Flexibility and adaptability are key traits of successful advocates. If a particular approach proves ineffective, being able to pivot and try alternative methods can make all the difference. For instance, if a social media campaign doesn't generate the expected engagement, shifting to in-person community meetings might be more effective. Learning to pivot ensures that advocacy efforts remain dynamic and resilient in the face of challenges.

Effective Use of Media and Social Platforms

Leveraging media and social platforms is a powerful strategy for reaching wider audiences and amplifying advocacy messages. Understanding and effectively using these tools can significantly enhance the impact of advocacy efforts.

Utilizing traditional media involves engaging with newspapers, television, and radio to disseminate advocacy messages. These long-established channels have a broad reach and can attract significant public attention. To maximize their potential, advocates should develop strong relationships with journalists and editors who cover relevant topics. This can be achieved by regularly providing valuable information, offering exclusive stories, and being a reliable source of insights on the issues at hand. Additionally, submitting op-eds or letters to the editor can help insert your message into public discourse. Appearances on television and radio shows further extend your reach, offering opportunities to present your advocacy messages directly to a diverse audience.

Harnessing social media is another crucial component of modern advocacy. Platforms like Twitter, Facebook, and Instagram offer unprecedented access to large audiences and enable direct engagement with supporters and critics alike. Creating compelling content is key to capturing attention on these platforms. This includes crafting visually appealing graphics, writing clear and concise posts, and using hashtags to increase visibility. Engaging with followers through comments, shares, and likes helps build a vibrant online community. Consistent posting and leveraging trends can keep your audience engaged and informed. Social media also allows for real-time updates and rapid response to emerging issues, making it an indispensable tool for contemporary advocates.

Conducting media outreach focuses on establishing strong connections with journalists and media outlets. Building these relationships requires regular communication and the ability to pitch stories that align with both your advocacy goals and the interests of the media outlet. Crafting press releases that are newsworthy, clear, and concise is essential for capturing the attention of busy journalists. Press releases should include a compelling headline, a succinct summary of the issue, and quotes from key stakeholders. Organizing media events, such as press conferences or media briefings, provides a platform for delivering your message directly to multiple media representatives. These events should be well-planned and executed, ensuring that key messages are conveyed effectively.

Measuring media impact is vital for understanding the effectiveness of your advocacy efforts and refining your strategies. Tracking media coverage involves monitoring mentions of your advocacy in newspapers, television segments, and online articles. Tools like Google Alerts and media monitoring services can help keep track of this coverage. Analyzing social media metrics, such as likes, shares, comments, and follower growth, provides insights into how well your messages are resonating with your audience. Understanding which types of content generate the most engagement can inform future social media strategies. Adjusting tactics based on these analyses ensures that your advocacy remains dynamic and responsive to the changing media landscape.

To create compelling messages, focus on clarity and conciseness. Clear messages are easier to understand and more likely to resonate with audiences. Avoid jargon and complex language; instead, use simple and direct phrasing. Personal stories and anecdotes can make your messages more relatable and impactful, but they should always serve to clarify and reinforce your main points. Tailoring messages to your audience is also crucial. Understand the values, interests, and concerns of different groups and adjust your messaging accordingly. For example, what resonates with university students may differ from what engages community leaders or previously disengaged citizens.

Summary and Reflections

This chapter equips readers with essential tools and strategies for effective advocacy. It covered the importance of understanding the advocacy landscape at various levels—local, state, and national—and provided insights into mapping stakeholders to identify allies and opponents. By setting SMART goals, advocates can create clear and actionable objectives that align with community needs. Developing detailed action plans ensures tasks are well-organized and resources efficiently allocated. Evaluation of advocacy efforts through both quantitative metrics and qualitative feedback allows for continuous improvement.

Readers also learned how to utilize public speaking and persuasion techniques to craft compelling messages, engage audiences, and handle objections. Building strong coalitions by identifying partners, leveraging collective resources, and maintaining motivation is vital for greater impact. Understanding the political context and tailoring communication strategies to different terrains enhance the effectiveness of advocacy efforts. Finally, mastering the use of traditional media and social platforms amplifies advocacy messages, reaching wider audiences and driving meaningful change.

CHAPTER 8

Sustaining Engagementand Taking Action

Sustaining engagement and taking action in civic involvement is a path filled with opportunities to make meaningful contributions to communities. By maintaining consistent participation, individuals can drive positive change and address pressing social, political, and environmental issues. Engagement must be thoughtful and continuous, requiring deliberate planning and the willingness to adapt strategies as needed. This chapter aims to provide readers with practical steps and insights into sustaining their involvement over time while making tangible impacts on the issues that matter most to them.

Readers will explore how to develop a personal civic engagement plan, starting with identifying core interests and setting clear objectives. The chapter will cover methods for creating effective action plans that balance daily activities with broader community goals. Additionally, it will delve into the importance of incorporating community objectives into personal efforts, ensuring collective impact. Strategies for establishing accountability mechanisms, such as regular progress reviews and support networks, will also be discussed. By following these guidelines, readers will learn how to sustain their engagement and take action effectively within their communities.

Developing a Personal Civic Engagement Plan

To achieve sustained civic involvement, it is essential to begin by identifying your personal civic goals. The first step in this process is to reflect on the issues that resonate most with you. Ask yourself what social, political, or environmental matters you feel passionate about. Is it climate change, education reform, or social justice? Identifying these core interests will help you focus your efforts and ensure that your actions are driven by genuine concern.

Once you've pinpointed the issues that matter most to you, the next step is to set specific, achievable objectives. Rather than aiming for broad, ambiguous goals like "making a difference," try to be as precise as possible. For example, if you're passionate about environmental conservation, your objectives could include reducing plastic waste in your community, starting a local recycling program, or advocating for stricter environmental policies at the municipal level. Clear, focused goals not only make your efforts more manageable but also provide a sense of direction and purpose.

After establishing your objectives, it's time to map out an action plan. This involves combining daily actions with broader community objectives. Start by breaking down your larger ambitions into smaller, manageable tasks. If your aim is to improve local education, consider volunteering at a nearby school, organizing book drives, or mentoring students. Daily or weekly actions, such as participating in community clean-ups or attending city council meetings, can gradually build toward your bigger goals. An effective action plan ensures that your efforts remain consistent and aligned with your long-term objectives.

Incorporating community objectives within your individual action plan is equally important. Engaging with local organizations, attending town hall meetings, and collaborating with other activists can amplify your impact. By working collectively, you can address larger systemic issues that require communal effort. For instance, joining forces with a neighborhood group to push for safer pedestrian crossings will likely yield better results than working alone. Remember, effective civic engagement often hinges on collective action.

To ensure you stay on track, establishing accountability mechanisms is crucial. One approach is through personal reflection. Regularly assess your progress and adjust your strategies if needed. Keeping a journal can help track accomplishments and identify areas for improvement. Additionally, setting up periodic reviews, perhaps monthly or quarterly, allows you to evaluate whether you are meeting your objectives.

Another method to maintain accountability is to create support networks. Surrounding yourself with like-minded individuals who share your passions can provide motivation and encouragement. These networks can include friends, family, colleagues, or members of local advocacy groups. Peer accountability can be especially effective; for example, forming a study group to learn about local governance or pairing up with a buddy for volunteer activities can keep you motivated and committed.

Creating a timeline for your engagement is another essential step. This involves scheduling your civic actions, volunteer opportunities, and educational pursuits while balancing them with your personal commitments. Start by setting short-term milestones that lead to your long-term goals. If you aim to become a board member of a local nonprofit, begin by attending their events, volunteering, and making connections within the organization.

Your timeline should also account for varying levels of engagement. Some periods may allow for more intense involvement, while others might require scaling back. During busy times, focusing on smaller, manageable actions like signing petitions or writing letters to representatives can keep you engaged without overwhelming your schedule.

Balancing engagement with personal commitments is key to sustaining long-term participation. Overcommitting can lead to burnout, diminishing your ability to contribute effectively. Striving for balance ensures that you can maintain both your personal well-being and civic responsibilities. For instance, allocating specific hours each week for civic activities while reserving time for self-care prevents feelings of being overwhelmed.

Educational pursuits play a vital role in your timeline. Continually learning about the issues you care about, whether through reading, attending webinars, or enrolling in relevant courses, enhances your knowledge and efficacy as an activist. Stay informed about current events and developments related to your interests to adapt your strategies accordingly.

Continuing Education and Skill Development

Sustaining civic engagement demands ongoing effort and dedication, and one of the most effective ways to maintain this involvement is through lifelong learning. Young adults, university students, community leaders, and previously disengaged citizens can all benefit from continuously developing their skills and knowledge in order to become more effective advocates.

To start, identifying relevant training opportunities is crucial for anyone looking to enhance their civic skills. Workshops, webinars, and courses that focus on aspects such as public speaking, policy analysis, and community organizing can offer invaluable insights. These educational sessions often provide practical tools and strategies that can be directly applied to activism efforts. For instance, a workshop on grassroots campaigning might teach participants how to effectively mobilize volunteers or communicate their message to a wider audience. Many universities and local organizations offer these opportunities, making it easier to find training that fits your schedule and interests.

Engaging with mentors and role models is another vital aspect of sustaining engagement. Building relationships with experienced activists and community leaders can provide guidance and inspiration. Mentors can share their own experiences, offering advice on navigating challenges and achieving goals. For example, a seasoned activist might share strategies they used to successfully lobby for policy changes or tips on maintaining motivation during long-term campaigns. Regular meetings and discussions with mentors can also help in crafting a clear, focused approach to advocacy work. The shared wisdom and support from these relationships can be instrumental in personal and professional growth within the civic sphere.

Participation in civic discussions and forums is equally important. These platforms provide a space to engage with diverse perspectives and stay informed about current social issues. Attending town hall meetings, panel discussions, and online forums allows individuals to hear different viewpoints, ask questions, and contribute their thoughts. This active participation helps in honing critical thinking and debate skills, which are essential for effective advocacy.

Furthermore, these interactions can lead to networking opportunities, connecting individuals with like-minded peers and potential collaborators. Engaging in meaningful dialogue not only broadens one's understanding but also strengthens the collective impact of community efforts.

Another significant component of lifelong learning in civic engagement is reflection. Regularly assessing your actions and experiences enables you to identify areas for growth and improvement. Reflecting on both successes and failures provides valuable lessons that can inform future efforts. For instance, after organizing a community event, taking time to evaluate what went well and what could be improved can lead to more effective planning and execution in the future. Keeping a journal or engaging in group reflections with peers can facilitate this process, making it easier to pinpoint specific strategies that worked and those that didn't. Reflection encourages continuous learning and adaptability, which are key traits for sustained involvement and advocacy.

Additionally, creating a timeline for engagement can help maintain momentum and ensure consistent participation. Mapping out a plan that includes short-term and long-term goals, alongside regular check-ins to assess progress, can keep individuals on track. For example, setting monthly objectives such as attending a certain number of workshops or volunteering hours can provide structure and motivation. This timeline can also incorporate personal milestones, celebrating achievements and recognizing the hard work put into civic activities. A well-organized approach makes the process of staying engaged less overwhelming and more manageable.

Success Stories and Lessons Learned

To inspire sustained civic involvement, examining real-life examples through case studies of effective civic initiatives plays a pivotal role. One such example is the community-led project in Flint, Michigan, where locals responded to the water crisis. Residents banded together to demand clean water and accountability from their government. By organizing public meetings, distributing bottled water, and creating awareness campaigns, they successfully pressured officials to take action. This story offers a relatable template: identify the issue, rally the community, and maintain persistence.

Analyzing this case helps us understand the strategies that can be adapted to different contexts. For instance, the use of social media to amplify messages proved crucial in Flint. Activists posted updates, shared stories, and created hashtags to keep the issue in the public eye. Such strategies can be useful when addressing environmental issues, advocating for educational reforms, or tackling other community-specific challenges.

Interviews with seasoned activists provide another layer of authenticity and valuable insights. Imagine learning from someone like Alicia Garza, co-founder of the Black Lives Matter movement. In her experience, building a successful movement involves not only passion but also careful strategizing and resilience. Interviews with experts like Alicia highlight the importance of understanding both the struggles and the triumphs inherent to civic engagement. These personal anecdotes enrich our knowledge by showing practical application of theories and plans.

Engaging with these experts allows readers to hear firsthand accounts of the long hours, the setbacks, and the small wins. For example, an activist might share how they handled pushback from authorities or navigated internal conflicts within their group. These stories remind aspiring activists that obstacles are part of the journey, and overcoming them is central to achieving goals. Each interview becomes a beacon of hope, illustrating that determination and strategic thinking can lead to impactful changes.

Common obstacles faced by activists often revolve around limited resources, burnout, and resistance from those in power. Addressing these challenges requires effective strategies. Resource limitations can be mitigated by forming alliances with other organizations that share similar goals. Collaboration not only pools resources but also broadens the support base, making it easier to mobilize larger groups for actions or events.

Burnout among activists is a significant issue due to the emotional and physical demands of their work. To combat this, it's essential to promote self-care and mutual support within activist communities. Techniques such as rotating responsibilities, taking regular breaks, and providing mental health resources can sustain long-term engagement. It's important to remember that sustaining the individual is as critical as sustaining the movement.

Resistance from authorities and opposition groups is another hurdle. Employing non-violent communication techniques and negotiation skills can help navigate such confrontations. Additionally, documenting interactions meticulously and seeking legal advice when necessary ensures activists are prepared to defend their rights and actions if challenged.

Celebrating small victories is crucial for maintaining morale and promoting positive momentum. When activists only focus on end goals, the path can seem daunting. Recognizing incremental progress helps sustain engagement by showing tangible results along the way. For instance, a community group aiming to improve local parks might celebrate milestones like securing initial funding or completing a first round of tree planting.

These small wins should be both acknowledged and shared publicly. Organizing events or using social media to highlight achievements can attract new supporters and reinforce the commitment of existing ones. Celebrations not only bolster the spirits of those directly involved but also create broader awareness and excitement around the cause, drawing more people into the fold.

By breaking down large goals into smaller, manageable tasks, activists can create a sense of continuous achievement. Each completed task serves as a stepping stone toward the ultimate objective, maintaining enthusiasm and commitment over time. This approach not only sustains momentum but also builds a record of success that can be leveraged for further advocacy efforts.

Building Community Connections and Networks

Fostering stronger community ties and collaboration among civic-minded individuals is essential for creating lasting change. One effective way to do this is by exploring methods to connect with local organizations and groups that share similar civic interests and goals.

Begin by identifying what issues you are passionate about, such as environmental sustainability, social justice, or educational reform. Once you have pinpointed your interests, use online resources like community bulletin boards, local newspapers, and social media to find organizations aligned with these causes. Attending events hosted by these groups is a great way to meet like-minded individuals and learn more about their initiatives.

In addition to joining existing organizations, forming coalitions and alliances can significantly amplify your impact and resources. By working together, groups can pool their expertise, volunteers, and funding to tackle larger projects and advocate more effectively for their causes. For example, environmental groups might join forces with educational institutions to create comprehensive sustainability programs in schools. When forming a coalition, ensure that all parties share common goals and establish clear communication channels to coordinate efforts and resolve any conflicts that arise. Regular meetings and updates will help keep everyone informed and engaged.

Organizing and attending community meetings, town halls, and public forums are critical techniques for fostering collaboration and engagement. Start by researching when and where these events take place in your area. Local government websites, community centers, and libraries often provide information on upcoming meetings. To make the most of these gatherings, come prepared with questions or topics you wish to discuss. Engaging in dialogue with elected officials, community leaders, and fellow citizens provides valuable opportunities to voice concerns, share ideas, and develop actionable plans.

Moreover, if there are no existing forums addressing your concerns, consider organizing your own. Reach out to community members and local organizations to gauge interest and secure a venue. Promote the event through flyers, social media, and word of mouth to attract participants. Facilitate open and respectful discussions, ensuring every attendee has a chance to contribute. Documenting the outcomes and action points from these meetings helps maintain momentum and accountability.

The use of social media and digital platforms offers significant advantages in creating virtual communities and support networks. Platforms like Facebook, Twitter, and Instagram enable individuals to connect with others who share their civic interests, regardless of geographical constraints. Create or join groups dedicated to your causes, participate in conversations, and share relevant content to build awareness and enthusiasm. Digital tools like Slack, Discord, and Zoom facilitate real-time communication and collaboration, making it easier to organize virtual meetings, webinars, and workshops.

When leveraging social media for civic engagement, it is crucial to maintain a balance between raising awareness and taking tangible actions. Sharing informative articles, videos, and infographics can educate your audience and inspire them to get involved. However, don't forget to encourage offline activities such as attending local events, volunteering, and advocating for policies at school board meetings or city council sessions. Use social media to promote these actions and celebrate the successes achieved by your community, reinforcing the sense of accomplishment and shared purpose.

One powerful aspect of fostering collaboration is celebrating small victories along the way. Recognizing and appreciating incremental progress keeps morale high and motivates continued efforts. Whether it's organizing a successful neighborhood cleanup, securing a meeting with a local official, or reaching a fundraising goal, take the time to acknowledge these achievements publicly. Share these milestones on social media, highlight them in newsletters, and give shout-outs during meetings to build a culture of encouragement and positivity.

Utilizing Technology for Civic Engagement

Leverage technology to enhance civic engagement efforts and reach broader audiences with these strategies.

First, let's delve into the digital tools and apps that facilitate effective communication, organization, and collaboration among activists. With the proliferation of smartphones and internet access, various applications have emerged that make it easy for activists to coordinate their efforts. Apps like Slack and Microsoft Teams enable real-time communication and project management. These tools help in setting up virtual meetings, sharing documents, and managing tasks among team members regardless of their locations. They create an environment where ideas can be exchanged quickly, issues can be addressed promptly, and decisions can be made efficiently. Additionally, project management tools such as Trello or Asana allow activists to break down their goals into manageable tasks, assign responsibilities, and track progress. This level of organization ensures that every member knows their role, timelines are adhered to, and objectives are met effectively.

Next, let's discuss the potential of social media campaigns to raise awareness and mobilize supporters for various causes. Social media platforms like Facebook, Twitter, and Instagram have revolutionized how information is disseminated and how communities rally around causes. Through well-crafted posts, hashtags, and engaging content, activists can reach a vast audience within a short span of time. For instance, the #BlackLivesMatter movement gained global attention through its strategic use of social media, making it easier for people worldwide to connect with the cause and participate in related activities. Creating engaging content, such as videos, infographics, and live streams, can captivate audience interest and encourage them to take action, whether it's signing a petition, attending a rally, or donating to a cause. Additionally, influencers and celebrities can amplify these messages, lending their platforms to reach even wider audiences.

Moving on, we explore online platforms for petitions, crowdfunding, and other forms of digital activism. Websites like Change.org and GoFundMe have democratized activism by allowing anyone with an internet connection to start a campaign and gather support. Change.org, for example, enables individuals to create petitions that can attract millions of signatures, putting pressure on decision-makers to address specific issues. Crowdfunding platforms like GoFundMe and Kickstarter provide avenues for raising funds for initiatives, whether it's organizing a protest, creating educational materials, or supporting community projects. These platforms not only offer financial support but also build a sense of community among supporters who invest in the cause. Additionally, websites like Avaaz run global campaigns on issues ranging from climate change to human rights, showing how collective digital actions can lead to tangible impacts.

Addressing the importance of cybersecurity and digital privacy in civic engagement activities is crucial. With the rise in digital activism, the need to protect personal information and communication channels has become paramount. Activists often face threats from those opposing their cause, including hacking attempts and surveillance. Using encrypted messaging apps like Signal or Telegram can safeguard private conversations from unauthorized access. It's important to educate activists about strong password practices, two-factor authentication, and recognizing phishing attempts. Moreover, VPNs (Virtual Private Networks) can help activists maintain anonymity and secure their internet connections when browsing or participating in online activities. Ensuring digital security not only protects individuals but also maintains the integrity and confidentiality of the activist movements.

Final Insights

The chapter has provided a roadmap for developing a personalized civic engagement plan. By identifying personal goals, setting achievable objectives, and creating actionable plans, readers are equipped to make meaningful contributions to their communities. Emphasizing the importance of community involvement, the chapter highlights the value of collective action and collaboration with local organizations. Accountability mechanisms and support networks are necessary tools for maintaining long-term commitment, while managing personal commitments ensures sustained engagement without burnout.

Furthermore, incorporating educational pursuits within this framework reinforces the significance of continual learning in effective activism. Staying informed about relevant issues and developing new skills through workshops, mentorships, and forums empowers individuals to adapt and enhance their strategies. The chapter encourages balancing digital and offline actions to maximize impact, leveraging modern tools while fostering strong community connections. Altogether, these steps create a sustainable path for ongoing civic involvement, enabling readers to become proactive participants in shaping their communities.

CONCLUSION

Throughout this book, we've delved deeply into the essence of civic engagement and activism. We've outlined not just the importance but also the mechanics of getting involved in your community and making a meaningful impact. As we reach the end of our journey together, it's essential to take a moment to reflect on the key lessons we've learned and how they can pave the path to effective civic participation.

One defining takeaway from our exploration is that civic engagement forms the heartbeat of democracy. Informed activism empowers us individually and collectively, providing the tools necessary to shape a better future. We discussed various aspects of activism, emphasizing that knowledge equips us, while action transforms that knowledge into tangible change. From understanding our political landscape to identifying issues that resonate personally, the foundation has been laid for you to play an active role in your community.

Empowerment begins with education. Throughout this book, we've stressed the significance of being well-informed about social issues and the political environment. This knowledge is crucial because it provides the context needed to identify where change is most needed and how one can best contribute to those efforts. Understanding legislative processes, recognizing the roles of different civic bodies, and being able to critically analyze social issues are integral parts of informed activism.

Yet, having knowledge is only part of the equation. The true power lies in applying what you've learned. The real measure of civic engagement is not just in understanding but in action. Now that you have the tools and resources, take a moment to envision your first step. Whether it's attending a local council meeting, starting a petition, or volunteering with a nonprofit organization, remember that action is the bridge between knowledge and change. These initial steps may seem small, but they lay the groundwork for more significant endeavors. Civic engagement often begins locally, with small actions that build momentum over time.

Moreover, the journey of civic involvement doesn't end after taking the first few steps. It's a lifelong commitment that requires sustained effort and continuous learning. Civic engagement is not a sprint but a marathon. Just as a gardener tends to their plants season after season, your ongoing dedication to your community will yield growth and renewal over time. By staying informed, continuously educating yourself, and remaining active in community affairs, you ensure that your efforts remain relevant and impactful. This long-term perspective is crucial because the challenges faced by communities often evolve, requiring adaptive and ongoing strategies.

Think of your role in civic engagement as being akin to nurturing a living organism. It requires patience, care, and persistence. There will be moments of triumph and setbacks, yet each experience contributes to your growth and effectiveness as an activist. The importance of resilience cannot be overstated; challenges and obstacles are inherent in the path of social change, but they also offer opportunities for learning and improvement.

As we conclude, it's vital to inspire the next generation of activists and leaders. Imagine being the spark that ignites change in your neighborhood. Your journey of activism can set an example for others; by sharing your passion and experiences, you can cultivate a movement that thrives on collective effort. One of the most powerful aspects of activism is its ability to inspire others to join in. By communicating your story and involving others, you create a ripple effect—one person's effort can galvanize an entire community.

Consider the stories shared within these pages, tales of ordinary individuals who took extraordinary steps to drive change. Their journeys serve as a testament to what's possible when passionate people come together with a common goal. You too can become a beacon of hope and a source of inspiration. Engage with schools, community centers, and social groups, spreading the message that civic engagement is essential for a thriving democracy. Encourage discussions, organize workshops, and facilitate events that inform and motivate others.

Remember that leadership in activism is not reserved for a select few. Each person has the potential to lead in their way, whether by organizing events, speaking publicly, or working behind the scenes to support initiatives. Effective leadership in activism also involves mentoring others, sharing knowledge, and fostering an inclusive environment where everyone's contributions are valued.

Finally, let this book serve as a reminder that the power to effect change lies within each of us. Civic engagement isn't confined to the politically inclined or socially adept; it's a space where everyone, regardless of background or expertise, can make a difference. The tools and strategies discussed throughout this journey are at your disposal, ready to be wielded in the service of community and country. Embrace this responsibility with the confidence that your actions, however small they may seem, contribute to a larger mosaic of progress.

In closing, I urge you to take the lessons learned here and apply them vigorously. Embark on this journey with enthusiasm and determination. The world needs dedicated individuals like you to champion the causes that matter most. Every meeting you attend, every petition you sign, and every conversation you initiate plants a seed for future change. Together, we can build stronger communities, foster greater inclusivity, and create a society that truly reflects the values we hold dear.

So go forth, informed and inspired. Let your activism not just be a chapter in your life but the very narrative that defines your legacy. The path ahead is challenging, yet profoundly rewarding. Step confidently into the role of an engaged citizen, ready to leave an indelible mark on the world. The future of activism starts now, with you.